War At Sea: A Canadian Seaman On The North Atlantic
Lugus Publications

War At Sea
A Canadian Seaman On The North Atlantic

by

Frank Curry

Lugus

Published by
Lugus Productions Ltd.
48 Falcon Street
Toronto, Ontario
Canada
M4S 2P5

Canadian Cataloguing In Publication Data

Curry, Frank
    War at sea

ISBN 0-921633-52-1

1. Curry, Frank. 2. World War, 1939-1945 -
Naval operations, Canadian. 3. World War, 1939-
1945 -Personal narratives, Canadian. 4. World
War, 1939-1945 - Campaigns - Atlantic Ocean.
I. Title.

D811.C87 1990   940.54'5971   C90-093547-2

Contents

Preface

One evening, in the 1950s, I was in the basement of the United Church in Aylmer, Quebec, for a men's club dinner. The minister was making sure that we all met some of the newcomers, including a recent arrival to the area; a man with a German accent. He told us he was a recent immigrant from Germany; that he was working at odd jobs and looking for regular work; and that he and his family had been lucky enough to find a place to live. Like many immigrants from postwar Europe, he was not letting his difficulties curb his enthusiasm for his new life in Canada with his family. He was eager to talk about the future, and not at all reluctant to discuss the past.

We got to talking, and inevitably, the war came up. He told me he had served in the German army as a gunner in coastal anti-aircraft batteries, including those set up along the French coast. As we continued to compare notes, it became clear to us that we had crossed paths during the war. We finally zeroed in on the location.

My new friend had been stationed on the cliffs overlooking the ancient seaport of St. Malo. As German armies were driven inland after "D-Day", many troops were left behind to hold fortified strong-points, including St. Malo. It was here that he manned his gun, guarding St. Malo and keeping watch on the sea approaches to this port, from which Jacques Cartier sailed in 1532, on his voyage to the New World.

While my friend kept watch, H.M.C.S. Caraquet and her flotilla were operating in the area, along the coast. We were sent toward St. Malo to rescue any crew who might have survived the crash of an American B-17 bomber, shot down by anti-aircraft fire in the approaches.

From my friend's perspective, it was a matter of watching the ships gradually come into view. They were clearly carrying out a search. He could see us very well, but he knew that we were out of range.

From our perspective, it was a matter of watching the gunners, as they occasionally let off short bursts to make us realize that they knew we were there. We knew their fire couldn't reach us, and we were able to continue the search with a minimum of worry about attack. We finally found three of the airmen from the downed aircraft; they were floating in a life raft, and they were unharmed. Throughout the operation, we kept close watch on the cliffs, making sure we kept out of range.

"We watched you too, very carefully," my friend recalled, describing the flotilla of Canadian ships, annoyingly out of range, but close enough to be an irritant.

What a strange thing war is!

The German gunner and the Canadian sailor, on opposite sides of the cliffs overlooking St. Malo, on opposite sides of the war, could never meet *then* in friendship. Yet here we were, *now,* in the warm atmosphere of a church supper, almost ten years later.

Here we were—*friends!*

My story is about the gulf that separated us for a while.

INTRODUCTION

World War Two drifts slowly into oblivion. Aside from academic histories by earnest historians, little more may be recorded about this conflict by those who were a part of it.

There have been very few accounts, that of Farley Mowat being a notable exception, of the wartime experiences of a Canadian private.

As for the Canadian navy, I do not know of a single account of life below decks in our fleets of destroyers, corvettes, fairmiles, sweepers and cruisers. Passing reference has been made to the 100,000 young men and women who joined the navy, but their real stories remain lost: stories of those who manned the ships, fired the guns and depth charges, took on the challenge of submarine detection, maintained and ran the engines, fought the battles ashore on shore patrols, lugged the ammunition and stores aboard, manned sea boats, cooked, tended the sick and wounded (doctors served only on the few large ships), jumped buoys, and lived for years amidst filth, ice and water, reaching starvation levels of subsistence, eating hardtack when the last mouldy loaf of bread was gone.

By chance (and against the rules) I kept a diary of my experiences throughout more than five years in the navy. This document rests in splendid isolation in the National Archives of Canada. Other journals recorded by fellow-sailors would have helped me flesh out the bare bones of my own recollections. Yet, rough and sparse as my diary entries often were, I'm thankful, now, that I persisted.

Over the years, I shaped these recollections into this book which I hoped would re-enact the experiences of an *ordinary* Canadian seaman.

I know that any attempt to recall events and experiences decades after they happened, even with the valuable aid of a diary, is subject to all kinds of distortion and exaggeration. Conversely, a glimpse of the distant past can often provide considerable enlightenment. Which of these polarities is more pronounced in the pages that follow will be the reader's decision. For myself, I only know that I have tried to provide the view from the lower deck. Not only for myself, but, I would like, for all other seamen, stokers, engine-room artificers, gunners, torpedo men, sick-bay attendants, signallers, wireless telegraphers, cooks and wardroom servants; the 100,000 of us who served aboard wartime ships under wartime conditions.

Part One: H.M.C.S. Kamsack

A Prairie Boy Joins The Navy

I grew up in Winnipeg, Manitoba, thousands of miles from both the Pacific and Atlantic Oceans. A prairie boy, through and through. And yet, like thousands upon thousands of others, from the farms, villages, small towns and cities of the prairies, I ended up on a corvette in the North Atlantic.

In my late teens, I folIowed every development in Europe in the late 1930s with a frightening intensity. My ear glued to our small radio, I took in every speech of Hitler, every word of political commentators and politicians. Unlike my father and eldest brother, who told me that I was taking it all too seriously—that there would be no war; that Europe would find a way out of it without war—I sensed a terrible doom approaching. Even as I was enjoying the independence of my first job, in the summer of 1939, handling correspondence for officers in the Royal Canadian Corps of Signals, the letters I was dispatching indicated that war was imminent. I had no idea what *my* role would be.

It was purely an accident that landed me in the navy. The outbreak of war in September found me in Ottawa, a capital in the throes of mobilization. The streets were jammed with young people, pouring in by the thousands to fill new wartime jobs. Social life became an explosion. I remember the Saturday night dances in Hull, which lasted well into Sunday morning.

It was a curious life. Three times a week, I would get decked out in my sailor's outfit and, for a few hours, take on the role of a sailor on a dry-land ship, H.M.C.S. Bytown. There was endless drilling, marching, and forming a gun's crew around some ancient twelve-pound naval gun which must have come down from the Battle of Trafalgar. And there was lecture after lecture on seamanship from grizzled old petty officers, who told shattering tales of life in the peacetime navy—how this sailor and that sailor had had his leg sheared off by a wire hawser. He reminded us, again and again, that we were fortunate to be part of the inland navy.

The experience left me perplexed: would I ever become a real sailor, battling the elements and the enemy? Was I going to spend the rest of the war as a part-time sailor on a dry-land ship? I had learned the drill: put in a request to see the commanding officer and ask for immediate active duty. And the next time the request list came up, I was on it. I marched up, saluted, and told the high-and-mighty three-ringer that I had joined the navy to be part of it, and was now so requesting. The officer glared at me, hinted that I was impudent, then told me that I would be put on active service in three days: "Dismiss, about turn."

Facing my civilian boss wasn't nearly as easy. He was furious: who was I to make such decisions on my own? Didn't I know that I was in a protected position? But when I said that it was my last day, all he could do was to throw up his hands. He knew he couldn't stop me. I was bound for active service with the Royal Canadian Navy. But I didn't know that the sea, the ships and the war were still far away. All that I had to prove I was a sailor was the uniform. Bell-bottom trousers, jumper, singlet, traditional flat hat bearing the insignia H.M.C.S. (Her Majesty's Canadian Ship), lanyard, and Canada badges on each shoulder. All my civilian gear went back to Winnipeg: it would be more than five years before I saw it again.

I found my way to naval headquarters in downtown Ottawa, and reported to a chief petty officer, who told me I was to join the navy patrol responsible for guarding wartime secrets; that I would be armed with a loaded rifle and bayonet; and that, as the newest of new recruits, my hours of duty would be midnight to 8 a.m. (or 0800 in the service). My patrol area would be the back alley behind naval headquarters.

"So much for fighting the war at sea," I grumbled to myself. The tedium of patrol duty was something to grumble about. Night after night, I stumbled into the alley to face eight hours of darkness, silence and loneliness. These eight hours felt like eternity. The only sounds were the occasional yowl of a cat, or the almost silent footfalls of the duty petty officer, perhaps hoping to catch me off guard, maybe asleep.

I made friends with the duty petty officer who took over at 0800 hours. He was a good head, and didn't look upon a recruit as some kind of dogsbody. We became friendly. One morning, he asked me if I would like to see the *inner sanctum* of naval headquarters.

For the first time, I was given a glimpse of Canadian naval activities in the North Atlantic. There were rooms filled with wall-size graphs showing the locations and courses of Canadian convoys and German U-boats. In this brief exposure to a graphic documentation of the war at sea, I think I realized, for the first time, the dimensions of what was going on. How inadequate and insignificant I was in all of it. It was like the difference between the back alley and the real war, even though it was represented on wall boards.

This insight made the nights interminable, deadly, depressing. After some weeks of this agony I knew I had to do something. I put in a request to see the commanding officer, asking for a draft to the naval training headquarters in Halifax. To my delight, my request was granted. "Dismiss, about turn."

I had three days before leaving for Halifax: not much time to pack my kit bag, say my goodbyes, pick up my travel warrant, and head for the old Union Station. It was while I waited for the train, amidst the throngs of uniformed men bidding farewell to wives or sweethearts, I felt, finally, I was on my way to the real navy.

The journey was a new experience. I fought my way on board the train, all the seats grabbed by the more experienced travellers, for the short ride to Montreal. There the scene was more chaotic. An eruption of laughter and smiles, tears and pathos, drunks, cursing clods and scared-looking teenagers. Every shade of young Canada prepared to board the Maritime Limited. I suppose there were others like myself; alone, and overwhelmed by the emotion of the farewell, the uncertainty of the future. I clung to my kit bag and travel warrant, and inched toward the train. The few military police did their best to keep order in the midst of chaos—the shouting, cursing, tears of separations. Finally I managed to squeeze into the end of a coach.

This wartime train to Halifax from Montreal was something out of Kafka. It revealed how quickly all the niceties of peacetime can become raw. There remains little room for human behaviour. This was a train alive with the activities of war: drunkenness, cursing, boisterousness, laughter, noise, song, and the mournful melodies of a harmonica. Never a quiet moment. During the stops men jumped off to find whatever food they could. I am sure we left some of them behind. I tried to accept the madness of it all. I hoped that it would soon come to an end.

At one a.m. we came to a stop. Tired, hungry and confused, I searched for a friendly face. No one came to my aid.

The crowd slowly thinned; at last I could see a sign. A check-in point for new arrivals.

The petty officer glanced at my travel warrant, pointed into the pitch dark, and told me to climb aboard a truck. Transportation to my ship! H.M.C.S. Stadacona. Once again a land-locked vessel!

Soon, I had joined a dozen other arrivals for the bouncy ride down Barrington Street, cobblestoned main street of Halifax. The surroundings looked miserable. When we arrived, not a single person was there to greet us. We stood in the rain, gazing at the long, low buildings with their dim exterior lights. Welcome to the East Coast navy.

From Raw Recruit To Submarine Detector

Inside the block-long barracks of H.M.C.S. Stadacona, the dim night-lights revealed row on row of wooden tables and benches; above them, hundreds of hammocks, slung inches apart, tight against the ceiling. A solitary sailor on fire watch moved slowly between the rows of hammocks. I decided to curl up and try to sleep.

At 6 a.m. the tranquillity was shattered by the voice of the duty petty officer who, armed with some kind of club, marched through the barracks, hammering the bottoms of hammocks and screaming at the top of his lungs. He was bellowing a call to rise in a rhythmic sing-song. It started with an invitation:

"Come on, my hearties..."

What followed was a string of expressions characteristic of the navy penchant for strong language.

7

Soon, he had the entire barracks stirring, muttering and offering their own rude rejoinders. Few men lingered. Slithering out of their hammocks, they lashed and stowed them in a matter of minutes.

I was issued my hammock later that day; it was to accompany me, along with my kit bag and pay book, throughout the war.

For the next hour, the barracks was a madhouse. I joined one of the lineups leading into each of the washrooms, and managed to capture a wash basin. Then came breakfast. What a shattering experience! The cook-houses were attached to one side of the barracks, and the food was issued in pans; twelve portions to each table. Fair enough, except that everyone but me seemed to have an allotted table. I watched the food disappear, not knowing how to break into the charmed circle. To add to the uproar of banging plates and clanging silverware, half the sailors in the barracks headed for two old-fashioned milk cans slung in the middle of the floor. A free-for-all developed: milk was splashed everywhere. A fortunate few ended up with a cup of the precious liquid. I stared in bewildered astonishment. This was navy life?

All I can offer by way of explanation for such wild scenes is that the navy may have decided to expose us to the tough realities right from the start. Whatever the reasons, my introduction to H.M.C.S. Stadacona, the main East Coast training barracks, left me confounded and lost. While everyone else seemed to be part of a group, I drifted, wondering if I would ever find safe haven.

For my first few days, I drew k.p. in the kitchen. From then on my waking hours were spent peeling potatoes and onions, scrubbing pots, washing dishes, cleaning and polishing. Breakfast duty began at 0500 hours, with the preparation of monstrous pots of porridge, pan after pan of red lead and bacon (greasy bacon with canned tomatoes), huge platters of bread and endless vats of tea. I hardly had time to look around and size up my surroundings. I managed to make out the layout of the barracks: huge, flat buildings, side by side, on a hill overlooking the dockyard and harbour, which stretched east to the open Atlantic and west into Bedford Basin,

where the convoys formed. I could even catch glimpses of naval ships tied up at the docks, and moving in and out of harbour, as well as an endless parade of merchant ships, flying all the colours of the world. These sights, brief as they were, gave me a sense of the sea, the ships, the war.

But I would have a lot to learn before my involvement became more direct than a view of the harbour from my barracks. Luckily, my first lesson was a pleasant one: comradeship. I was ordered to join a large draft of new recruits from Montreal, and I soon became part of this boisterous, lively group of English-and-French-speaking Montrealers from all walks of life: Polish-Canadians, Jewish-Canadians, upper-class Montrealers, working-class youths from St. Henri. Most were about my age—barely out of their teens—with a handful of older men (all of thirty years old!) and even a few married men. I quickly made friends with several of the Montrealers, and one of them, John Granda, became a very close friend. Throughout the war, John and I spotted each other in different ports, and waved from fo'c'sle to fo'c'sle when our ships passed close to each other.

Our days were filled with hours of marching, drilling and wheeling in and out of formation on the enormous parade square in the dockyard. Slowly, we developed from awkward squads to cohesive marching groups;

forming fours, swinging into line, sizing, slow-marching, marching with rifles and fixed bayonets, and following the bellowed orders of the chief petty officer in charge of our group. Woe to anyone who broke up the parade drill or was caught smirking or talking: he soon found himself lugging a heavy naval shell up and down the hill for hours.

But there was much more to our training than the parade square: long hours on the rifle range with ancient Lee-Enfield rifles; day after day in seamanship classes, being drilled in knots, splices, wires and ropes, and names of parts of a ship; lookout drills; aircraft recognition; gunnery drills; more days out in Halifax harbour to learn to handle naval cutters and whalers, boat's crews and sailing rules, coming alongside, hoisting and lowering, and jumping buoys. It was during this initial exposure to boats and the water that we had our first close-up view of tragedy: one of our groups, with a veteran petty officer in charge, found its whaler tangling with a merchant ship, one of a long line of ships forming an outbound convoy coming out of Bedford Basin. The whaler was crushed, and the petty officer, entangled in the wreckage, went to the bottom of Halifax harbour; luckily, the others made it to shore. It was with an understandable reluctance that we later obeyed our training officer's orders to jump, fully clothed, into deep water; and to try to stay afloat while being dragged down by the weight of our thick navy uniforms.

As the weeks passed, we no longer felt like total civilians in a naval setting. We were still dry-land sailors: not one in a hundred of us had ever been aboard a ship, let alone across the Atlantic. But we were slowly preparing ourselves to serve aboard naval ships, although some of our experiences on dry land made getting to sea seem far away.

One of the many initial shocks for civilians moving into the military way of life is the anonymity of huge barracks after the warmth of family life. I was no exception, as I contemplated the dreariness of Stadacona's block-long, wooden, single-storey buildings, each of which became the home of hundreds of young men. In surroundings with the minimum of comfort, we slept, ate, washed, wrote letters, chatted, complained, listened to the mournful music made by Halifax cowboys, and lined up for our pay once a month. Every Saturday was spit-and-polish routine, when we had to make the barracks presentable to the officer of the day, who, after inspection, barked out the requisite:

"Any complaints?"

And received the requisite reply: silence.

Life in such a setting was never peaceful. There were long lineups, to wash; to eat; to use the bathrooms. It was almost impossible to find a quiet corner in which to write a letter, since the tables were usually occupied by participants in the strictly verboten crap games so popular with many of the men. Reading was only possible in the last hour before lights out: you slung your hammock, crawled in, and hoped to have enough light to make out the words on the page. There was never enough space. Hammocks virtually rubbed each other along the steel bars running the length of the barracks. Gear was stowed in small wooden lockers down the middle of the building. (What we didn't realize was these conditions were luxurious in comparison to the seaman's mess on a corvette).

Mealtime was something else. Twelve sailors to a mess table, with one man designated to mark off helpings on the mess pan. I learned after my first meager breakfast to make sure I got my fair share, especially if I was one of the last to be served. Rule number one: if you weren't aggressive, you went hungry.

We were all assigned to one of three watches (red, white and blue), which meant that every third day (and night), we drew some form of extra duty. After a long, tough day of training, after the evening meal, the whistle was piped and the duty watch mustered. There, lined up, we were handed some choice activity: clothesline sentry, perhaps. An odd-sounding activity, but essential for prevention of wholesale theft of our gear from the clotheslines alongside the barracks.

Then, there was security sentry, which meant walking, armed with rifle and bayonet, along a high fence topped with barbed wire, and circling the entire perimeter of the barracks. It was a lonely business, especially if you drew the midnight-to-four watch. After the late-night duty, it was close to impossible to get any rest before the jarring wake-up call at 0600. (If you were lucky, there was some relief, in the form of a hot cup of tea furnished by a kind-hearted cook, himself up at four to start breakfast.)

There was also the fire watch, inside and outside the barracks. It was a key precaution, since the wooden buildings were tinder-boxes. If this wasn't enough, there was also kitchen duty: peeling vegetables, cleaning pots, and helping to get the next meal ready.

Six days a week, the Halifax navy was separated into its various barracks, with no contact between us. On Sunday we all came together on the parade grounds to march; column on column we formed up, square after square, until the grounds became a sea of blue uniforms: sailors, ready for Sunday services and the dreaded inspection before the top brass. The naval band played familiar sailors' hymns and songs. "For Those in Peril on the Sea" and "Hearts of Oak" were big favourites.

Everyone was expected to be in tip-top shape for the inspection: shoes polished, uniform clean and spotless, hat at the proper angle, bows tied correctly, face clean-shaven and hair at regulation length. After the brass had looked us over, it was then the turn of the veteran master-at-arms. He always looked all too ready to jot down the name and number of any unfortunate sailor who had failed to shave closely enough, or had placed his hat at the wrong angle.

It was always a relief when the Sunday drill was over; although, in retrospect, I can recall that there was a surge of camaraderie as we looked around the great gathering of sailors, all ready and willing to head off to war, and to realize we were a part of it all.

Evenings off found many of us lined up for inspection by the duty officer, turning in our I.D. cards, and promising to behave on the streets of Halifax, to be back on board by 0700 hours. For married men who had brought their wives to Halifax, it was a welcome reunion; for the others, it was a chance to do the town, to wander aimlessly in streets jammed with sailors, soldiers and airmen; to have a meal in the Bon Ton (a favourite beanery); to line up in front of the Capitol Theatre; and, at the end of the evening, to make the long trek down cobblestoned Barrington Street, fending off bootleggers; to check into barracks, hoping to find a spot to sling your hammock.

Weekends were even more prized, since we could "go ashore" after 1300 hours on Saturday and Sunday, and explore the city and environs in daylight, swim in the Northwest Arm, wander in the lovely Point Pleasant Park, visit the famous Citadel Hill and Town Clock, catch the Dartmouth ferry and make our way to the Dartmouth lakes. We could walk through ancient burial grounds to find gravestones linked to many sea tragedies, including the sinking of the Titanic. At night, there were the dances. Tough competitions, with an average of a dozen sailors to each girl.

One evening, when I lined up with the other duty-watchers, I stepped forward expecting to draw fire watch, or clothesline watch. Instead, I was ordered to report to the wet canteen in the dockyard to serve beer and wash glasses. It was one of the few places in Halifax where beer was legally available to the thousands of sailors from all parts of Canada.

I set off for the naval dockyard filled with curiosity and just a little apprehension. I was still under the age of majority; I had never been inside a tavern or beer hall. The canteen was more than just a first glance at beer-drinking. The war had, so far, been a remote event for me: I had caught glimpses of warships and convoys heading out to sea, and others making their way into port; once or twice I had seen some famous British battleship, or the Queen Mary, heading down Halifax Harbour for the open Atlantic and Britain. It was the wet canteen which made the experience immediate.

The canteen itself was a long, low room, dimly lit, with a serving counter at one end, and tables and chairs jammed into the remaining space. As soon as the doors opened, sailors poured in from ships and barracks and the beer began to flow. It was served in big, thick glass mugs. In no time, the canteen was filled with noisy sailors downing beer as fast as it could be drawn from wooden barrels. The tales flowed with equal ease. Sailors home from the sea, with dry land once again under foot, loosened their tongues in comradeship, telling and re-telling experiences at war.

For me, it was an overwhelming experience: I was outside the circle, a green recruit who had yet to put a foot aboard a ship, yet caught up in this world of sailors and their lives. I hardly knew what to think.

The chief petty officer in charge of the "wets" had no doubt what to do about me. He gave me the job of turning on the spigots, filling the mugs to overflowing, and lining them up on the serving counter. At the same time, I had to dip and rinse dozens of empty mugs which had returned from the dark recesses of the canteen. Fill, fill, fill; wash, wash, wash. It was like working on a Charlie Chaplin assembly line, racing to keep up with the insatiable demand for more beer, right now. The tough old chief was very understanding. He urged me on, reminding me at the same time that I was free to consume as much beer as I wanted. It was a wasted opportunity (I had yet to discover the joys of beer-drinking) and a source of shock to the chief, who was astounded that there existed a sailor who could be sur-rounded by an ocean of beer and not take the plunge. (I made up for this slow start later in my naval career!)

At midnight, we cleared the glasses and butt-filled ashtrays, and straightened all the tables and chairs ready for the onslaught the following evening. I finally headed off up the hill, alone with my thoughts. My mind was filled with the life of the canteen, and I wondered when I, too, would be heading ashore off a ship, and searching for the "wets" or some other respite.

There was one curious turn to this tour of duty: for some reason, the old chief must have taken a liking to me, since I had quite a few duty-watch assignments to the wet canteen. As it turned out, the experience made a deep and lasting impression on me, for it reflected all the human feelings of men trying to find, even for a few hours, some meaning in all the uncertainty of war. I could understand all the uproar and singing, the oaths and tales. Here was the war, brought ashore to a dimly-lit building in the naval dockyard; and even as I drew beer and washed mugs for all the other sailors, I sensed that I would soon share some of the experiences they were describing.

Whether they were demanding, exciting, or simply trying, there finally came a time when all the weeks of training on dry land led to a first experience at sea.

One evening, our Montreal draft was told that we were to have our first close look at a naval ship the following day. We were to proceed in groups of twenty to the naval dockyard, and from there to go aboard one of the river-class destroyers just back from convoy operations in the North Atlantic. We reacted with great enthusiasm: we were one step closer to the real thing—a ship of our own.

Off we marched the next morning, through all the bustle and confusion of the dockyard, to the destroyer wharf, where our ship lay tied up. She was an imposing sight, with her patches of rust and salt, her wartime camouflage, and the crew swarming all over her decks. No doubt that this was a ship back from the wars, with ample evidence of her life at sea. We gaped at her 4.7 twin naval guns, her anti-aircraft turrets, her rows of depth charges, her crew lugging fresh supplies aboard, cleaning their ship, and readying her for a return to sea. We dry-land sailors were more than awed at coming this close to a fighting ship, and as we stood waiting to go aboard, I wondered when we too would be sailors on such a ship. But even before we could cross the gangway and step aboard, we were faced with the inevitable barrier: no sea-tested crew welcomed an invasion by a group of raw recruits. As we put foot on the steel deck and approached the crew, I felt an intense coldness from the men on board. The stares, the looks of disdain, the rejection, were abundantly clear. We were invading their ship, their sanctuary. They wanted no part of us.

Subdued, uncertain, we trooped our way from top to bottom. In and out of mess-decks, up on the bridge, down to the magazines, into the engine room. Everywhere we came into close but silent contact with the crew of this fighting ship. We were reminded that we were outsiders, that this ship and its close-knit crew would just as soon have us depart at the double.

We suffered silently under this pall, stumbling through narrow hatchways and confined mess-decks, through a maze of passageways, past humming machinery and gear, deep into the bowels of their ship. It was with relief that we completed our tour and headed across the gangway, back to the friendly confines of our barracks.

Our next experience with a sea-going ship, days later, finally brought us in contact with the harsh reality of the sea itself. Our training petty officer said we were going aboard H.M.C.S. Beaver, a millionaire's cruise yacht, which had been donated to the war effort and was now a training ship of the Canadian Navy. We headed off into the early morning darkness, marching through the dockyard and clutching bags of bologna sandwiches, our food rations for this first day at sea.

The Beaver looked rather small and insignificant after the river-class destroyer we had previously boarded. Long and slim, she was hardly the image of a fighting naval ship fit for the North Atlantic. She had one twenty-pound gun mounted on her bow. But she carried depth charges on her stern, since she had to be ready for any eventuality. German U-boats had been known to operate in the approaches to Halifax harbour, and even a training exercise might involve the real thing. No chances could be taken.

We were assigned various duties, mostly as lookouts, and then the small permanent crew took over the key roles. Soon the Beaver was on her way down the long confines of Halifax Harbour, past the Halifax-Dartmouth ferry, past McNab's and George's Islands, past Porter's Island, and past the gate vessels marking the outer reaches of the great harbour. We were all eyes, and full of talk, this our first day on a ship heading for the open Atlantic. What a moment for a prairie boy who had never been on a ship; who had never had a glimpse of an ocean!

Once out of the gates and off Chebucto Head, things suddenly changed. The sea didn't appear to be rough on this early winter day, but the Beaver started to do strange things in the long Atlantic swells: her bow dipped deep into the icy seas, then rose sharply to the blue skies overhead; heavy sheets of spray broke over the bow and were flung high over the bridge—a fabulous sight the first few times. As the heaving and dipping continued, all the chatter and laughter stopped, and a subdued group of dry-land sailors discovered that ships pitch and toss, roll and twist; and that sailors experience first-hand all this rolling, pitching and tossing. Every nuance of the ship's movements is shared by the crew, and with not entirely pleasant results. Gone in an instant was that romantic, idyllic image we had brought with us. We learned that going to sea was going to be hell for most of us. What's more, we were learning this lesson while hardly out of sight of Halifax harbour, on the first day aboard our first ship at sea.

Many of us were soon deathly sick, and even the boldest ones, who tried to look cheerful, seemed green around the gills. Our duties were to be carried out regardless of our condition, and this made the outlook grim. We were united in a single purpose: to get through this first day of training at sea, and head for the safety of the harbour and the jetty. Lunchtime came, but very few could bear the thought of eating the thick bologna sandwiches. The afternoon seemed to drag on forever. At long last, the captain turned H.M.C.S. Beaver toward land. Slowly we came abreast of Chebucto Head and into the lee of the land, protected from the Atlantic swells. All the pitching and tossing subsided, and the ship came alive with our voices once more. We were now anticipating the finest moment for all sailors of all ages: returning to port; tying up alongside; and basking in the most precious moment of seafaring life — stepping onto *terra firma*.

We had been to sea. No longer were we dry-land sailors. Soon, we all knew, we would be going our separate ways to join ships and become part of the war. The navy had endeavoured to give us the training required of a seaman aboard ship. We would be expected to stand watches; be lookouts; handle ropes and wires; lower, raise and handle sea boats; fight fires; react to such disasters as collisions; act as quartermaster on the wheel under certain conditions; and carry aboard food, supplies, ammunition and depth charges. The standard duties of a seaman in the lowest rank in any navy.

War At Sea: A Canadian Seaman On The North Atlantic

The Canadian Navy had more training in store for some of us before we became part of a ship's crew. While quite a few of my group were handed their first draft to ships in Halifax, or sent to man the new ships coming out of Canada's wartime shipyards, many of us were given the option of more specialized training; for example, on the ship's guns, torpedoes and depth charges. Yet another option appealed to me: to become involved in ASDIC, the recently developed and highly secret means of detecting submarines. The name was derived from Anti-Submarine Detection International Committee. ASDIC was based on the principle of sending out a narrow sound beam which would bounce back a sharp echo if it encountered any underwater body, particularly a large metallic object like a submarine. Various equipment measured the distances, movements, speed and manoeuvres of the detected object; recorded the echoes and provided the timing and required ship's movements leading to the firing and dropping of depth-charge patterns. These would, with the proper time settings, explode on and near the submarine, damaging or destroying it underwater, or forcing it to the surface to face further attack.

I volunteered for ASDIC training and was accepted, joining a group of seamen from across Canada, some of them from my old Montreal draft. Little did I realize that this decision would take me to the very heart of the war at sea. I would be detecting submarines, mines, on convoy operations; and protecting our merchant ships, their crews and their vital war supplies, in all parts of the North Atlantic and the English Channel. Barely out of our teens, we were to be handed responsibility for the safety of ship and crew, and of up to eighty other ships in convoy. We were expected, during every moment of an ASDIC watch, to probe the ocean's depths knowing that the next transmission might bring the dreaded echo of an enemy submarine less than 3000 yards off the port beam.

Our fellow-sailors treated us with a mixture of respect and contempt. Many were the remarks that we were going "ping-happy" (a reference to the "ping" of the transmissions which hammered us every few seconds, with presumably disastrous effects on our mental faculties), yet we sensed that our comrades knew their lives depended on us, for all our limitations and inadequacies. If we failed to detect a returning echo after a transmission, a U-boat could destroy our ship, even the convoy.

The ASDIC training program covered little about U-boat warfare, strategy, tactics or philosophy. From the day we signed the document committing ourselves to ASDIC for the duration of the war, I cannot recall a single lecture, discussion or paper about the war at sea and our part in it. We were left entirely out of the big picture, expected merely to absorb training and carry out our duties to the best of our abilities.

The training to convert us into submarine detectors (S.D.) was intensive, beginning with a thorough run-through of the theory of ASDIC, and the equipment developed to apply the theory. The earliest equipment consisted of a large, flat, round transmitter which would be lowered or raised inside a dome fastened to the keel of the ship, directly under the bridge. In a compartment surrounding the transmitter and dome, the transmission equipment, powered by high-speed motors, created the sound beam, sent it out through the transmitter, and, at the same time, carried it to the operational gear (high on the bridge, in the case of corvettes).

The submarine detector's job was to control the transmissions sent out every few seconds on a sweeping arc. We were taught to use earphones to follow the sound of the transmission out to its limits, 3000 to 4000 yards under ideal conditions, and to listen intently for any sign of an echo. An echo was the ultimate sound of danger: the trigger for action stations; the start of attack procedures leading to the firing and dropping of 150-pound depth charges in patterns aimed at the conning tower of the attacker.

As well as echoes, we were expected to listen for any sound of engines or motors, since the transmitter also acted as a receiver for any sounds in the ocean's depths.

We spent weeks getting used to the equipment, and then faced what would become the bane of every S.D. in the navy—the attack table, a sophisticated (and monstrous) mock-up of a convoy operation, including escort ships, columns of merchant ships and attacking U-boats plus a variety of weather conditions and water variations. These were manned by a veteran group of ASDIC staff members, including Commander Welland, the top anti-submarine expert in the Royal Canadian Navy. They drove us young and inexperienced recruits to the breaking point. Commander Welland created impossible situations; wreaked havoc; drove us to tears by screaming and yelling at our mistakes and breakdowns. He seemed determined to come as close as possible to the combat situations we would all face when isolated aboard a destroyer, a corvette or a bangor. It was a fearful and soul-destroying introduction to the war at sea before we ever put a foot aboard an operational ship. For the rest of the war, in whatever naval port we found ourselves, all the ASDICs spent every hour in an attack-table bus, hammered and harrassed with every new element of ASDIC operations. We spent week after week in the ASDIC school, and many of us felt we were caught up in an impossible situation. There was no backing out: we were in it, for better or for worse.

Finally came the day when we took our classroom knowledge to sea. Off we set for St. Margaret's Bay, down the coast from Halifax, and aboard an ASDIC-equipped training ship. In the vast peace and calm of this magnificent bay, we joined a Dutch submarine for ten solid days and nights of manoeuvres against a German U-boat—simulated by our Dutch ally. It dodged and wheeled in the depths, shutting off its engines and sitting silently on the bottom as our ASDIC transmissions tried to establish contact.

Contact was made...the attack began...the charges were dropped...contact had to be maintained...contact was lost! We were subjected to scathing criticism from Commander Welland as we continuously blundered our way through the procedure. Finally, a brief word of praise for a correct manoeuvre.

Some evenings, the Dutch submarine tied up next to us, and the crew invited us to come aboard and explore their home. Closing the conning tower hatch, they took us for a dive, and allowed us, with glimpses through their periscope, to view the world as seen from a cruising submarine.

The end of our training came, along with a brief closing ceremony in which we were told that we were now considered qualified S.D.s and could sew a distinguishing badge on our uniforms.

Back we went to H.M.C.S. Stadacona barracks to await a draft: our close-knit group realized that this was a parting of the ways, although, in the years that followed, we would cross paths in many parts of the ocean; in strange ports; and as our ships passed in the night. And we would also lose a number of our comrades in action.

Aboard H.M.C.S. Kamsack

Our training days were behind us. We had been on seagoing training ships which ventured out into the Atlantic from Halifax, and we were as ready as a wartime navy could make us, ready for ships of our own, ready to become part of the real navy.

Soon, we were mustered alongside our Halifax home, H.M.C.S. Stadacona, to hear our destinations: I was headed for Montreal; drafted to H.M.C.S. Hochelaga, the manning barracks at the foot of the Jacques-Cartier Bridge, just across the St. Lawrence River from downtown Montreal. We weren't given any idea of what would happen to us; we were sent to Montreal aboard the packed Maritime Limited with no berths or dining cars. Trucks met us at the station and dropped us at the gates of Hochelaga, where we scrambled to get a bunk, stow our gear, and settle into this barracks teeming with sailors.

Through the grapevine, we found out we would probably end up aboard one of the new escort ships, probably a corvette, the sturdy trawler-style vessel which was starting to arrive from Canada's wartime shipyards. When would we be assigned? Days? Weeks? No one had a clue. Days of impatient waiting, with little to do except carry out the make-work of picking up pieces of paper and cigarette butts with sticks armed with nails. Hardly my idea of sailing the oceans of the world.

We did have one enjoyable outlet. Early each morning, hundreds of us would form up in marching order and head off into the surrounding countryside, marching to the skirl of the bagpipes. I looked forward to this daily outing. Cheered on by farmers in the fields. Marching to all the familiar Scottish tunes was a joyful experience. The pipes shared in this happy coming together of sailors and soldiers.

We were free to explore Montreal two evenings out of three. I took every opportunity to make the walk across the Jacques-Cartier Bridge into the heart of Montreal. I walked everywhere, finding new avenues to follow; trying new foods; nursing my seaman's pay to make sure I didn't go broke.

One day, we were called together and a list of one hundred names was called, mine among them, to form the crew for H.M.C.S. Kamsack, a spanking new corvette of the Flower Class. She was built in Port Arthur, nudged down the Great Lakes, and now awaited her crew at the Oka Docks. An exciting moment for all of us. Realizing we were taking over our first ship, we gathered our kit bags and hammocks, and piled into open-back trucks for the drive to the docks.

The trip was not as brief as we had expected; our truck driver confused the Oka Docks with the small cheese-making village of Oka (with its famous Trappist monastery) miles out in the countryside north of Montreal. At first we paid little attention to what was happening; then, some of us began to realize that a corvette wouldn't be tied up in a small village. The driver continued his search. We became increasingly frustrated, bellowing out obscenities as we bumped along the back roads. Finally, we turned back. Someone had convinced the driver of his error. At last we were on the Oka Docks. There she sat, our first ship, H.M.C.S. Kamsack.

In wartime grey, flying a White Ensign (the tattered remains of which I still possess), lining her decks, were a crowd of yelling sailors, who had arrived earlier in another truck. Our shipmates-to-be gave us the roasting of our lives, and when they heard where we had been, wandering in search of the Kamsack among the cheese rounds of Oka village, their amusement knew no bounds. We late arrivals thought we would never hear the end of this start to our first day as members of the crew of H.M.C.S. Kamsack.

The rest of the first day was a strange and somewhat bewildering coming together of the ship and her crew. We were all types and sizes, we were very young, and we hailed from every corner of Canada. And we were all strangers, feeling our way, trying to overcome the reserve we felt for each other, the fear of our new surroundings. None of us could guess that in years to follow we would become a tightly-knit group aboard this 1200-ton, 150-foot ship; that we would make it, most of us, through the joys and heartaches which lay ahead. We numbered 110 seamen, stokers, engine-room artificers, signallers, gunners, SDs, electricians and cooks.

Towering over all of us was a magnificent Newfoundlander, a Naval Reserve officer, Lieutenant-Commander Randall, a World War One veteran called back from retirement to lead us into the unknown future.

We were mustered on the dock alongside our new ship. In a few words our captain went through the commissioning ceremony: we would make our way to Halifax, and from there join the fleet and the war.

After this introduction, thirty-five of us made our way to a small seaman's mess, no larger than a good-sized living room, right forward under the upper deck. Stokers were piled in below us; the engine room crowd behind and below us; the signallers, coders and cooks away aft. And the officers in private cabins with bunks.

The Kamsack remained tied up this first night. We took over our ship, inch by inch, finding our bearings, standing watches, readying the ship and ourselves for our first venture. She was far from being a fighting ship. Before our departure for Halifax we were equipped with depth charges and ammunition. We had our first experience of slinging hammocks aboard ship, and, at the quartermaster's orders, stowing them away by 0500 hours. While most of Montreal was still asleep, we pulled away from the Oka Docks: there were no bands; no cheering crowds, only one or two dockyard maties to slip our lines. In the early morning darkness we moved slowly under the great Jacques-Cartier Bridge and pointed our bow east down the broad St. Lawrence.

We were all in it together: veteran fishermen, merchant seamen, landlubbers from the offices of Montreal and Toronto, Prairie farmers, West Coast lumbermen, bakers, even a Maori merchant seaman from New Zealand who had left his ship in Montreal and joined the Canadian Navy.

It was a gentle introduction to life aboard H.M.C.S. Kamsack. We headed down the mighty St. Lawrence. Ancient strips of farms, from early seignory days, stretched back from the river on both sides.

The waters were calm. We stood our watches in the warm sunshine. Life was indeed pleasant. The navy wasn't such a bad place after all. At Sorel the river broadened into Lac St. Peter and we sailed on, the shores of the St. Lawrence far off on both sides.

We continued to follow the buoys and markers, keeping to our proper way down river. Ships of all kinds moved in each direction. Late in the evening, we spotted the heights of Quebec. I marvelled at the fortress-like ramparts. I picked out the Chateau Frontenac; the walled city of Old Quebec. Soon we were tied up for the night.

I was duty watch and missed the chance of going ashore to explore the city. Come midnight, I became duty quartermaster on the gangway, checking the late arrivals. I kept a watch on our lines ashore, having been warned that there would be variation in the tide—twenty-four feet! No one in the school in Halifax had prepared me for this.

The tides dropped like an elevator. I could barely keep up with the slackening of the lines. I could see the Kamsack turning turtle because of my error. I managed until 0400, and gladly turned over the responsibility to the new quartermaster. It was a rude awakening to the new and unexpected roles which faced a green seaman, still far from the Atlantic and the war.

The following morning, we cast off and continued down the St. Lawrence; past Ile d'Orleans, which marks the widening of the river into the start of the Gulf of St. Lawrence.

Soon we could barely see the shores. Settlements became more and more remote, and we were seeing an area that was little changed from the days of Jacques Cartier as he described it in the 16th century:

"A great, endless and magnificent waterway, by far the mightiest river we have ever seen...amazed at the vast numbers of whales, large grey seals and porpoise-like belugas."

On and on we sailed, past Rimouski, where German U-boats were later to prowl and sink outbound merchant ships; past Matane; to the lee of the island of Anticosti astride the Gulf of St. Lawrence.

There was now a different motion to the ship. It no longer rolled gently, but began to dip and rise, roll and sway in the rougher waters.

Our sailing orders were to keep close to land on this our maiden voyage. When we reached the outer reaches of the Gulf on the Gaspé we continued to lay no more than fifteen to twenty miles off shore.

We headed down the eastern coast of the Peninsula, past the coast of New Brunswick, across the Gulf to the outside reaches of Prince Edward Island and into the narrow waters between Cape Breton Island and mainland Nova Scotia. In the pitch dark of midnight we felt our way through tricky waters, past Port Hawkesbury and across the waters of Chebucto Bay. Finally, we turned out into the Atlantic.

Our forays during training had given us an insight into what lay ahead: seasickness! It was when the Kamsack had cleared the Straits of Canso and Chebucto Bay and pointed her bow out into the wild Atlantic that we began to face a reality which was to become a familiar, terrible experience.

Heavy seas met us head-on. Kamsack started to rear and plunge, digging her bow into one oncoming wave after another, burying the fo'c'sle under masses of icy, frothing water. The sea roared over the length of the ship, filling the port and starboard passageways waist-deep, sending sheets of glistening spray over the bridge. Sea water shot into mess decks and into the galley. One moment we were buried and waterlogged; then the trawler design came through and our bow rose to the skies.

As the waters were thrown aside we were freed, momentarily, to ride crazily over the next great wave sweeping down on us. Once more, our bow dug deep into this mass of water and we went through another series of plunges, rolls, and contortions. The ship seemed to handle this but the crew was another matter. We quickly discovered that fighting the war at sea meant fighting for survival.

In this first bewildering encounter with winter seas it was not only the land-lubbers from Toronto, Ontario or Estevan, Saskatchewan who suffered the misery of the deadliest plague of the sea, seasickness. Even the hardened Newfoundland fishermen, who had many years of rough sea-going behind them, and the merchant seamen, who had sailed the oceans of the world in all types and sizes of ship, found the movements of the corvette overwhelming. Many of us soon succumbed to the pitching and tossing; in the first few hours everyone was sick, and got sicker. Mess decks were stinking wet holes.

After our duty watches, we were wet, cold, sick and faced with the impossible choice between our mess deck and an assault by the relentless ocean.

We did discover havens. One was behind the Kamsack's single funnel.

On the open top deck the funnel's broad back provided a measure of shelter. Some of the warmth from the engine room reached us through the vents. We became known as "The Funnel Gang." We huddled and commiserated, deadly seasick, unable to eat, dreading the next watch on the wing of the bridge or away aft.

The other spot that offered some refuge was under the short fo'c'sle break of our corvette, where two large coils of heavy rope were stored. Here some of us huddled atop the coils on our off-duty hours, our duffle-coat pockets crammed with hardtack—our only food for days to come. What a sorry lot we were! Sick, soaked, cold and utterly miserable. Somehow we struggled on, thinking of nothing else but to curl up and sleep. Realizing, inside, that we couldn't get away from the waves, or the sea-sickness, or ourselves: reality faced us. So did another endless day and night of experiencing the sea. The following day brought more of the same, and so did the third day. All we could do was to hang onto whatever kept us going: never a pause, never a break, never a moment of respite, just a sense, within ourselves, that it might relent, someday.

Although we all suffered, some men were affected more than others. One shipmate, a young French-Canadian from Trois-Rivieres, became sea-sick before the ship left port. He went on to suffer every time the Kamsack put out to sea, calm or rough. He had every right to ask to be put ashore as chronically seasick, but he was determined never to give an inch, and he took an awful beating. On the maiden voyage, during our first encounter with rough seas, he looked ready to die at any moment. He never admitted defeat, and he remained part of the Kamsack. He was an inspiration to all. A sadder case was that of a fifteen-year-old boy who was part of Kamsack's crew. Boy seamen were a carryover from the old permanent navy, the Royal Canadian Navy, and we fell heir to one. Our crew was mostly composed of young men, many still in their teens, with the one or two married men in their early thirties considered old. Our boy seaman, "Smith," made us all feel like old men. He had a high-pitched voice, a childlike face, and spindly limbs; he weighed 100 pounds. We wondered if he would be better off in high school instead of aboard a corvette in the North Atlantic. When he first landed on board, his almost angelic expression gave no hint that he had already mastered a most impressive range of foul navy expressions. He was as bold as brass, and ready to take on the whole navy, until we entered the heavy winter seas of the Atlantic.

Our boy seaman was reported missing from his watch. At first, it was feared he had been washed overboard (the fate of many a young Canadian wartime sailor), but luckily this hadn't happened. We finally found him in the bilges. He was covered with oil, pathetically seasick, more dead than alive. The first lieutenant carried him from his hiding place, cleaned and bathed him, put him to bed in his own bunk, and, over the following few days of rough seas, nursed the boy. Everyone on board, despite his own misery, felt a deep empathy for the youngster.

When at last we came in on Sambro Light off Halifax, and into the welcome protection of Chebucto Head, we had the wonderful feeling that only a sailor can experience. No more plunging, no more pounding, only the steady sound of engines carrying us to shelter from the cruel Atlantic. We had come through our first real test, and now we were veterans of the sea, or so we thought. As with one voice, a silent, morose crew suddenly became boisterous. Far cry from the sullen, despondent bunch of a few hours before. When we finally took the last few steps across the gangway to stand on dry land, we found one more new experience awaiting us. It was as if the land were alive, and had come up to hit our feet. We knew now what "finding your sea legs" was all about. The supreme joy of being home from the sea! The sailor's ultimate reward.

The fate of Smith? The schoolboy, who had been so tenderly nursed through our first encounter with the North Atlantic regained his jauntiness and his foul language. He resumed his role as the saltiest seaman on board the Kamsack.

After our maiden voyage the Kamsack was taken over by shore-based navy technicians and civilians. They swarmed from bow to stern, lugging aboard crates and boxes of gear and equipment. Every day, the Kamsack looked more and more like a warship. Welders were putting new gun mounts on the wings of the bridge to hold the latest in Orlikan anti-aircraft guns. The engines were given a fine-tuning by engine-room specialists; newfangled ASDIC gear and the echo sounder were pulled to pieces and tested repeatedly. Countless depth charges, each containing 150 pounds of high explosives and representing a major weapon against U-boats, were hauled aboard. Ammunition lockers were thrown open, block and tackles rigged, and magazines loaded with four-inch shells, star shells, anti-aircraft shells, pompom shells, cordite and fuses. (The ship was taken to an isolated wharf on the Dartmouth side to avoid a repeat of the collision of two ships in Halifax harbour in 1917, which caused such a tragic explosion.)

But that wasn't all. The food storage compartments were crammed with cases of bully beef, hardtack, canned vegetables and all the staples which were to keep us going for weeks. Precious barrels of 120 over-proof rum for rations were secured in the rum lockers; the liquor for the officers was stashed; the cigarettes and chocolate bars were stored in the canteen; and the few fresh foods—bags of potatoes and onions, loaves of bread, and fresh meat and eggs were stowed away in the galley lockers. There was even a bit of fresh milk, but it didn't last more than a few days. Before long, we would all get used to canned milk in tea and coffee, and to the old Royal Navy slab cocoa, kye, with its frothy thick coating of fat.

Kamsack then moved into Bedford Basin, at the end of Halifax Harbour, where outward-bound convoys formed up. Our vessel went through the process of "running the degaussing range." We tested the effectiveness of our degaussing gear—large electrical cables which encircled the ship and neutralized the magnetism of the all-steel construction, to protect us from German magnetic mines. While our ship took on gear, ammunition, stores, bundles of charts and secret code books, the crew was hauled ashore to continue intensive training in gunnery, signals, depth-charging, anti-aircraft drills, and enemy (and allied) aircraft recognition. For my group, it was day after day in the ASDIC base. The ship, too, was put through a transformation. New camouflage designs were added to her sides. We took off for all-day shoots off Chebucto Head, firing at a variety of targets including a moving drone towed by an aircraft. We found that our main armament, the four-inch naval gun up forward, shattered light bulbs inside, and triggered showers of insulation from our steel bulkheads. The chief electrician had his hands full tracing all the damage and making repairs to our electrical systems.

Finally the order came to proceed to Pictou, on Northumberland Strait, to begin operational work-ups. Ship and crew would undergo severe tests to establish whether or not we were ready for actual operations. I think everyone feared the ten-day operation, especially since the ship and the crew were still green. We were under the command of a senior officer and his staff, who kept at us twenty-four hours a day trying to hammer us into shape and give us a fighting chance to carry our load and survive.

We came to dread the next flashed signal from the shore-based head-quarters, ordering yet another bizarre task. There were anti-submarine attacks, ships' formations and manoeuvres, collisions, night operations, fire and rescue operations. We had to tow a damaged ship, shore up bulkheads, rescue a man overboard. When we dropped anchor, winding up a day which had started before dawn, there was the flashing signal from shore again. Our few hours of rest were shattered. Night operations!

Once or twice came the sudden command:

"Away sea boat's crew!"

After a mad scramble to man the falls and lower the heavy whaler to the water's edge, another command to let go the release gear; the whaler hit the water with a mighty splash.

I ended up with the seaman's boat crew, lined up with boats from other ships involved in the exercises. At the firing of a gun, everyone pulled mightily on the whaler's great oars as we set off on a demanding race of several miles around a distant buoy. Pictou harbour favoured us with calm, protected waters, and we didn't have to face the battering of North Atlantic swells and mountainous waves: that would come later. They were exhausting races, but we caught the spirit, and pulled for all we were worth, trying to cross the invisible finish line in front of the other four boats. Sometimes we did get there first.

The only real break came when permission was given to land the off-duty crews of the ships at the Pictou wharf. Several hours of freedom in this lovely town, long a haven for ships and sailors. It was an experience to land in a strange port for the first time. Soon we were crowding the few restaurants, looking for girls, and searching out some source of liquid refreshment. Many succeeded, as sailors have always succeeded, in locating the inevitable bootlegger and purchasing, at an outrageous price, a bottle of whiskey or rum.

When we all started to assemble on the wharf to await the return to our ships, a few of the more lubricated sailors began to sing, as sailors under the influence are wont to do. Soon, others joined in, and before long, the mass of young sailors took up the refrain. What singing! And what songs! These young volunteer wartime sailors had picked up questionable words to well-known tunes; familiar melodies took on an entirely new meaning as sailors roared out verse after verse of the foul lyrics. Those songs would never be the same again, and neither, I suspected, would the residents of Pictou! The boats arrived, tied to one another and hauled by a power boat. They hauled their raucous cargo back on board to sleep it off.

Following the final day of the operation, we were boarded by the formidable senior officer, a severe-looking four-ring captain with row upon row of battle ribbons. After a private chat with our captain and officers, he had the entire ship's crew assembled on the quarterdeck. He pointed out how inexperienced and ill-equipped we were to face the enemy. Grudgingly he allowed that we had reached a level of readiness that permitted him to clear us for operations.

With that, he gave orders for us to return to Halifax for assignment. After all the months of buildup and uncertainty, we were finally going to sea as a fighting warship and crew. Little did we all realize how truly unprepared we were to take on the North Atlantic and the enemy.

The Sydney-Newfie Run

It wasn't long before the Kamsack and her crew were bound for Sydney, Cape Breton naval base for operations. We headed into the North Atlantic, taking up continuous anti-submarine search, our piercing ASDIC operating continuously, night and day. I found myself trying to adjust to the demands of the notorious "two-and-four" routine: two hours of operating the ASDIC, followed by four hours off duty, and then the same again. And again.

Even during our off-duty hours, rest was frequently impossible because we were also expected to help maintain the ship. I was relieved when we made our way down the long confines to the Sydney base, with the glow of the steel mills and the fiery slag heaps as guiding beacons for our approach to safe haven. But we weren't left tied up alongside for long: after taking on last-minute oil and supplies, we received orders to join two sister corvettes and provide escort for an outward-bound convoy of merchant ships, which would join a main convoy from Halifax. The two convoys would meet at a rendezvous far off Cape Race, the most southeasterly point of Newfoundland, forming the last addition to the main body of the convoy, which had been collected at departure points along the east coast of the United States, particularly New York, Boston and Baltimore. This full convoy would proceed to Britain, or beyond.

Three escort ships, including the Kamsack, were to be responsible for about a dozen ships, flying the flags of a number of countries; all of them laden with war materials; tanks and aircraft lashed to their upper decks. The Kamsack, as the newcomer to convoy operations, was designated the junior ship; the least experienced.

The three ships moved out of Sydney, screening the outer approaches as the convoy gathered. I felt a part of the vast war at sea, however small a part. As I look back on those first few days and weeks of operations, one of my strongest memories is of the lack of information we ordinary seamen received about the war. The silent treatment was to persist throughout the war. For information, we were to rely on leaks, buzzes and rumours passed on by the communications group, the signallers, the wireless operators and the coders. Or, if we were in Halifax, we could go to the Bon Ton, a favourite restaurant and well-known to all sailors from the lower deck as a great source of first-hand information on convoys' sailing schedules, escort groupings, the comings and goings of individual ships, sinkings and attacks, and the various strategies planned by the Canadian navy. The rumours were rarely wrong.

On this first convoy, we knew little about what would happen until we

found ourselves off the approaches to Sydney and saw the dozen merchantmen formed up in three columns of four ships each; the senior escort ship ahead of the convoy, the second corvette in its screening pattern on the starboard wing; and the Kamsack formed up on the port wing, distancing herself three to four miles off the closest column of merchant ships. We immediately commenced our anti-submarine screening in a predetermined zig-zag pattern, lunging off to port for a set number of minutes, then wheeling to starboard, alternating the length of time and the distance in order to shield our pattern from any U-boats. For me and my fellow SDs, everything fell into place without any difficulty: Russ Telfer, Ron Cosburn and I beamed out our transmissions, 3000 yards every few seconds, listening carefully for echoes in our earphones as we trained the oscillator from abeam on the port side to dead ahead, then from abeam on the starboard side to dead ahead.

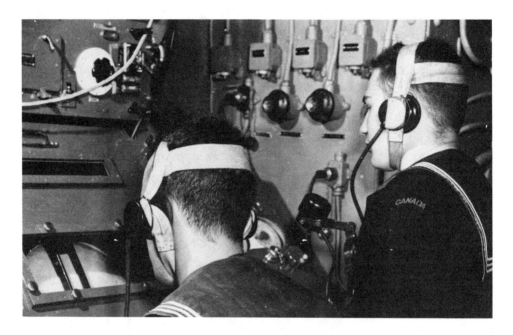

Our three ships, grouped in front and on two sides, zig-zagging and transmitting in prescribed patterns, were meant to provide maximum protection for the twelve ships. During daylight hours, being able to see the merchant ships made our jobs somewhat easier, but as darkness took over, and all the ships were blacked out, it was a different matter to keep the convoy shielded without running afoul of it. Station-keeping, particularly in the fog and storm, could become almost impossible. Ships could be scattered far and wide, some never to be rounded up, some sunk by marauding U-boats looking for easy prey. But on this our first try, we had no serious problems. Even in the darkness, we could make out the faint outlines of the nearest column of ships, and we continued our screening pattern without incident. The seas were far from smooth, but we ploughed ahead, toward our scheduled rendezvous, where we would meet the main convoy and the mid-ocean escort group.

The devastating enemy attacks near Canada's mainland, in the Gulf of St. Lawrence, up the St. Lawrence River and the east coast of the United States, were still to come. For the moment, attacks were mainly coming off Newfoundland, in the mid-Atlantic, off Iceland, and in all the approaches to the British Isles. As a result, we were not faced with the sudden torpedoing of merchant ships, the frightening rumble of a torpedo striking, the flames and sinking ships, ASDIC contacts and counter-attacks, the dropping of depth charges and the firing of star shells to illuminate the points of attack.

After days and nights of operating the ASDIC, grabbing something to eat in the galley, curling up for a blessed few hours of rest, meeting the first shades of dawn and the pitch black of midnight, never undressing, and hardly even thinking of washing or shaving, we began to close in on the rendezvous.

Far off Cape Race, the lookouts searched the horizon for hours, looking for some sign of the main convoy. Then, the first shout from the crow's nest: "Ships off the starboard bow!" (These were the days before radar.) Looming out of the darkness was a vast array of some sixty merchantmen, escorted by two destroyers and three corvettes: the mid-ocean escort group. There followed a rapid exchange of signals, and, at last, we felt the immense satisfaction of turning over our twelve ships, safe and sound, to the main convoy. After more exchanges, we made our farewells, turned toward port, and found we were ordered to proceed to St. John's, Newfoundland, at all possible speed. Our first operational assignment was complete.

Our small escort group of three corvettes headed at top speed (sixteen knots) for St. John's, taking up a line-abreast formation, ASDIC distance apart; as always, we were searching the depths for U-boats. Besides feeling we had accomplished something, we were looking forward to our first experience of tying up in a "foreign" port, the old and historic harbour of St. John's, which would not become Canadian soil until 1949.

We came up on the forbidding rock-bound coast of Newfoundland, the heavy seas of winter crashing wildly on the uninviting shores. Just where was St. John's? The coast appeared to be one unbroken barrier of rocky cliffs, snow-covered, towering far above us. Surely there couldn't be a large and safe harbour to be found anywhere around here. We slowed

down and took up a new formation of ships in line-ahead, with Kamsack on the tail end, then pressed ahead. All eyes were on the rough shores nearby. To our amazement, a narrow opening appeared, looking wide enough for only a very small ship. This barely detectable entrance to St. John's was soon nicknamed for obvious reasons, *The Neck,* or, *The Hole in the Wall.* We crept slowly through the narrow opening, and there, spread out before us, was the marvellous harbour of St. John's. Long and narrow. The Hole in the Wall was almost impossible to penetrate from any distance, yet one daring U-boat commander did succeed in firing several torpedoes which somehow made it into the outer reaches of the landlocked harbour. Once, one of our veteran river class destroyers ran directly into the rocky cliffs in the approaches to St. John's, tore her bow to pieces, and lost many of her crew. There was the old city climbing the snowbound hills on the right, and Cabot Hill and

its famous tower forever linked to Marconi and the first trans-Atlantic wireless message, high above the narrowest part of the entrance. We could spot heavy coastal guns on their mountings on both sides of the entrance, and, on the left, what we came to know as the South Side, with its battered old wooden houses and grim, sheer, rocky cliffs towering right up from the docks, covered in deep snow. There were ships everywhere: many were tied up on the main city side, but most naval vessels were tied up to buoys in the stream, or alongside on the South Side, four and five abreast. Several large oil tankers, including the Teakwood, which we came to know well over the years, were anchored in the stream, ready to service the fleet. Dominating the South Side was an ancient and decrepit wooden vessel, an old Clyde cruise ship now known as H.M.S. Greenock, the base ship which controlled the movements of both the Royal Navy and Royal Canadian Navy ships attached to St. John's Naval Base. It was impressive to us newcomers, especially when we caught sight of several merchant ships with yawning torpedo holes in their sides. One ship had sustained three such gashes, yet somehow had made it to port.

We found our spot at a jetty already four deep in corvettes, some of them rusty, battered and salt-encrusted, part of the mid-ocean group just back from a grim run to Iceland. Then began the mad rush to get the ship ready for sea again: opening all the portholes and compartment doors to get rid of the foul smells after many days at sea; scrubbing our mess decks; cleaning the ship from bow to stern; and getting rid of all our accumulated garbage. One welcome cleanup began after the fresh-water hoses from shore were hooked up to our water supply, and we were able to shower and shave for the first time since leaving Sydney! Meanwhile, fresh stores and supplies were lugged across four other ships, and a messenger scurried on board with sacks of mail; the navy had somehow forwarded it to St. John's.

The official word was that we would be in port long enough for two off-duty watches to go ashore. There was a mad scramble to change from shipboard gear and join the steady procession across the gangway. Unluckily, I drew the duty watch, and, with the other unfortunates, was kept trotting between the ship and sentry duty on the jetty.

To end up as jetty sentry, at midnight, in midwinter, in a total blackout, was not the choicest of duties. I found myself marching up and down in the darkness, my loaded rifle at the ready, greeting crew members returning aboard ship, and hoping for the end of the watch and a rest in my hammock. But sentry duty was much easier to take in warmer weather: during blueberry season, we jetty sentries stumbled over huge stacks of cases of the luscious fruit, ready to be loaded aboard ship. It wasn't at all difficult for one of us to slip a fourteen-pound box aboard where we all proceeded to gorge ourselves on the wonderful berries.

I did manage to get ashore for a short time, and find my way along the rough, unlit road on the South Side to the heart of St. John's, which was to become an important part of my life as home port throughout my service. As for the Kamsack's assignments, they would regularly take us between Sydney and St. John's, often escorting iron ore ships from Wabana, Belle Isle, to the steel mills of Sydney. Later, there would be anti-submarine sweeps off St. John's, or search-and-rescue operations involving ships which had been torpedoed, or separated from their convoys—choice targets for U-boats.

To begin with, the crew of the Kamsack was about to contend with her first exposure to a more fundamental difficulty: the North Atlantic in winter. It was a terrible awakening, as we headed out into the fury of winter gales, of icing, and of waves so massive and destructive that it took a lot of faith in our ship for us to believe that we could survive the constant battering and beating. But this faith was justified: the Kamsack was so well designed and strongly constructed that she survived all the Atlantic could do to us—although we did learn what it was like to have our lifeboats torn away from their moorings; carley floats flung to the hungry seas; depth charges wrenched from their wire lashings to roll around, crazily, as if weightless. It didn't happen to us, but it was not unknown for one of these charges to break loose, shattering some seaman's legs.

We had also heard tragic accounts of sailors swept overboard; torn away from the lifelines strung along the length of their ships, never to be seen again. As well, there had been ships, lost to "white mist," which plunged, with entire crews, to the bottom. "White mist" is a condition of icing in which the temperature suddenly drops to freezing, and the spray covering the ship instantly turns to ice. Within minutes, the ship is coated in solid ice, which, if it coats one side rather than both, can cause the ship to capsize. The might of the ocean in winter was overwhelming, and none of us ever forgot what it could do to us and our ship.

The tragedies of which we had been told didn't touch us directly, but we had our share of hardship, and were almost continuously battered, bruised, wet, weary, cold, sick and frightened; without hot food; our knee and hip joints screaming for relief from fighting the plunging and rolling of our ship. Watchmen and lookouts, soaked to the skin, their duffel coats thick with ice, had to peel off the coats and turn them over to the new watch. And on top of all this, we were somehow expected to be ready to take on U-boats and carry out all our duties at peak efficiency. This was the war at sea. The simple survival of ship and crew. The will to hang on, just above the level of despair. The strength to go on, hour after hour, day and night, until we reached port, a safe haven for ship and sailor alike. These were experiences to test and try us to the limits of our young lives.

Looking back, I think it was our youth and resilience that enabled us to absorb it all. Perhaps, if we had known that five more years of war at sea lay ahead, we might not have been able to cope. We will never know. Those first few months of operations in the North Atlantic in winter were forever washed deep into my bones, my being, never to be lost or forgotten, even all these years later. They tested me in a way which shaped my life, and my future.

Particularly tough on us were the urgent assignments, often far more demanding than escorting a dozen merchantmen in convoy.

One night, just back in our home port of Sydney, our tanks topped off, fresh supplies on board, our lines hardly ashore, we received an order to find and rescue a torpedoed ship in the Gulf. Out we went, at midnight, into the teeth of terrific seas. We were all desperately seasick. As I was making my way up to the bridge to take over my watch in the pitch dark of a winter storm, I stopped for a moment, clinging for dear life to the side of the wheelhouse. I must have been at least twenty feet above the water line, yet I still looked directly into the mountainous waves towering far above me on all sides. And these seas were to take us to a ship in trouble!

Somehow, our grand old man, Lieutenant-Commander Randall, did find the stray vessel, off St. Paul's Island. There was a huge torpedo hole in her side, but she was still afloat, and we were able to get a heavy tow line aboard her, turn about, and slowly make our way back to Sydney, and safety. For the first time, we had experienced the wonderful feeling of saving a ship and her crew.

We would also take away with us the less idyllic memories; the images of a mess deck knee-deep in foul sea water, spilled tins of jam, sailors' gear, hats, sea biscuits, letters and books.

Shortly after this rescue operation, and again in rough winter seas, we got a call to go to the aid of a fellow-ship, H.M.C.S. Grandmère. Her engines were down and she was wallowing in heavy seas. We found her, took her in tow, and once again were able to bring a crippled ship safely into Sydney. We had a great reunion with her crew, and shared in a rare moment of close fellowship.

Another tough assignment faced us one time in St. John's, in the depth of winter, the city hip-deep in snow, visibility near zero, and gale-force winds outside the snug and well-protected harbour. We set sail on one hour's notice, just before dawn, with orders to search for a torpedoed ship far off St. John's. There was a grim postscript to our orders: some of the crew had apparently taken to life rafts.

As soon as we headed through The Hole in the Wall we were met by the full fury of the North Atlantic. In pitch darkness, in the bitter cold, we plunged head-on into the oncoming waves, which broke over the ship from bow to stern. We were awash; decks and mess decks penetrated by the massive waves, and the crew a thoroughly miserable lot, sick as dogs, and praying for it to be over. We eventually found our way to the specified area and started the search, carrying out ever-widening sweeps, with all the crew on the lookout for the ship and crew. There was no sign of them. When all hope of finding any survivors was gone, our skipper made the decision to turn back, and we all knew that none of our fellow-sailors could have survived in the terrible conditions. It was an awful, helpless feeling of failure, a feeling we were to experience time and time again, each time we lost sailors and their ships to an Atlantic gale or an enemy torpedo. We had done our best, but it just hadn't been enough.

During the months that followed, we would learn more and more about ourselves, our successes and failures; our capacity to endure the punishing conditions, our closeness to one another; and, above all, our ability to cope with the North Atlantic in winter.

Our first winter at sea tested us greatly: the heavy, battering waves of the North Atlantic seemed never to cease their pounding or lose their destructive force. It was as if the very ocean was determined to drive our sturdy ship down. Sometimes, when we failed to break free from one mountainous wave, and remained buried in the trough, the next monster would crash down on us from high above, and for moments which seemed an eternity, it would appear that the Kamsack just couldn't recover, that she had more than met her match. She would be driven down to the depths, then she would rise, throw off the massive waves, and plunge into the next towering mass of icy water bearing down on us.

There were times when we drove into these winter seas head-on, almost sliding down the other side, as if riding a gigantic water slide. Often, we were so far down in the trough that entire convoys and their escorts disappeared from sight. There were other times, when the great waves came at us from directly astern, as following seas. Under these conditions, our small ship was tossed like a matchstick in a torrent, with each wave catching our stern and throwing us wildly out of control. The poor quartermaster on the wheel had the impossible task of keeping his heading on the true course as we swung crazily at the whim of the waves. As difficult as navigation became during these onslaughts, dealing with the waves astern was far preferable to the battering and beating we took when we faced the seas head-on.

As cold as the seas were, the air temperature was generally above freezing; as a result, the water simply rolled off us after working its way into every corner of the ship. But sometimes the air temperature dropped to freezing, or below, and this spelt potential disaster. If the seas were rough, with waves and sheets of spray constantly breaking over the ship, coat after coat after coat of ice would form, incredibly fast and without any warning. This was the *white mist* to which I referred earlier. It was a condition that we on the Kamsack experienced during our first tour of duty.

It happened just after we had brought our section of an eastbound convoy safely to its rendezvous with a main convoy far off Cape Race. Happy to have accomplished our assigned task, and even happier to turn about to head for our home base, we anticipated nothing more than yet another head-on battering from the waves. But, as the gale picked up and the skies darkened, we found ourselves separated from the other escort ships in our group, alone in the vastness and loneliness of the winter seas. Then, unknown to most of us, the temperature started to drop rapidly to below freezing, a rare event so far from land. The deadly combination of battering seas and sub-freezing temperatures soon combined to bring on what all sailors fear most—"white mist."

As the waves broke over us, great sheets of sea water and icy spray covered every inch of the ship, reaching the top of our tall mainmast. Sheets of ice rapidly formed over everything. Each crashing wave brought another coating of ice. As the waves broke in rapid succession, the layers of ice grew to alarming proportions. Nothing escaped the deadly process. On the fo'c'sle, our main armament, a four-inch naval gun encased in a heavy steel shield, took the initial brunt of the icing, and became a solid block of ice. This was only the beginning. The entire front of the bridge, high above sea level and the main deck, was one massive block of ice, feet thick. The foremast doubled, trebled, quadrupled in size, and the slender guy wires, stretching from the deck to the mast-top, were coated in ice a foot thick. In minutes, the relentless ice had formed over the sea boats, carley floats, depth charges, anti-aircraft mountings, guard rails, decks and gangways. Nothing escaped the "white mist." An even more dangerous development was in store for us. The seas, rather than hitting us head-on, were coming at us from off the port bow. Instead of having this enormous load of ice evenly distributed, our port side took the brunt of it, and we started to list strongly to port; the guard rails dipping further and further under the waves; the ship less and less frequently on an even keel. The implications were abundantly clear, our ship was succumbing to the elements. The fear of death was upon us.

The captain made no effort to hide the truth from us. We were in grave danger of capsizing from the sheer weight of ice, which was dragging our port side closer and closer to the point of no return; and that we must do everything in our power to free our ship from the deadly weight which would surely drag us to the bottom. Everyone pitched in, seamen, stokers, signalmen, even officers, to try to break the icy grip which was rapidly overcoming our ship. Our tools ranged from fire axes to sledgehammers, crowbars to old-fashioned belaying pins, steel bars to carpenters' hammers. Anything that was heavy enough to dislodge a chunk of ice. Even baseball bats, which we found in the ship's canteen, were added to the arsenal. It seemed we were fighting a losing battle. The ice continued to form, faster than we could dislodge it, and the waves and spray kept lashing over us. Hour after hour we fought it out, and a miserable battle it was for us, cold and sick as we were; wet and weary, driven by fear and fright. The aim of the struggle was simple but critical. We must keep the Kamsack upright long enough to reach port.

As fast as we sent massive chunks of ice tumbling into the sea, new ice formed in its place. Down the port side, the sea boat was torn away and dragged into the ocean by the sheer weight of the ice which encased it, and the Kamsack listed to port more and more, responding ever more sluggishly to our efforts to return her to something near an even keel. Again and again, we reminded ourselves of our goal: to make it to port. We kept up the battle against the white mist and crept slowly toward land.

Make it we did! At 0200 hours, we finally came into the lee of land off the long approaches to Sydney: there, we found respite from the gales and waves, and release from the deadly ice. The Kamsack crept silently down the harbour's long approaches and tied up in the silent naval dock. Hardly a soul was aware of our deadly struggle against the elements; even we ourselves could hardly take in the enormity of what we had undergone.

Later in the morning, as we struggled awake to see the ice-encrusted Kamsack sparkling in the brilliant sunshine, we were amazed to think that she could carry such a load and still stay afloat. We also felt, for the first time, the mystic bond between a ship and her crew; a bond achieved only through surviving the toughest challenges together.

We would see "white mist" in the years ahead, but we would never undergo an experience as fearful or, strangely, as rewarding as this one.

Convoy duties on the Sydney-Newfie run frequently took us into unknown waters and unexpected situations, not all of them involving the treacherous North Atlantic. On one mission, deep in winter darkness and heavy seas, we headed for Conception Bay, Newfoundland, looking for the settlement of Wabana and the iron ore docks of Belle Isle. Our orders were to escort three iron-ore ships to the steel mills of Sydney.

Because Belle Isle was deep in Conception Bay, it was difficult and dangerous to reach the ore docks; and the navy brass saw little danger of German U-boats getting at the docks and the ships with their valuable cargo of iron ore. But the navy brass was dead wrong, and the German navy did reach this supposedly impenetrable anchorage and torpedo several iron-ore ships loading at the docks. (Rumour had it that the U-boat was guided into the area by German merchant-marine officers who had, before the war, brought their ships into Wabana for iron ore.)

After this tragedy, the docks were protected by heavy anti-submarine nets: ships busy loading ore were safe enough in this haven, but once clear of Conception Bay, they were vulnerable to all the dangers of war at sea.

We crept into the loading docks in the pitch darkness of a winter's night. Apart from the shriek of the ever-present winter gale, the only other sounds were of the loading operations, which continued all through the night. We could see the dim outlines of the ships tied up at the docks, but it was impossible to see our surroundings as we tied up at the unlit docks, except for the sheer, towering cliffs of Belle Isle rising abruptly. A more desolate place was hard to imagine, but we were there for the night: the ships we were to escort wouldn't be ready to leave until early the next morning.

Despite the late hour, the darkness, and the uninviting winter winds, some of us were eager to venture ashore. It didn't matter what we did; just getting away from the ship, if only for an hour or two, would be a welcome break.

We decided to head for the little settlement of Wabana which, we were told, was some distance inland once we had reached the top of the cliffs which disappeared into the darkness above us. So off we set; a half-dozen of the more adventuresome among us. I have had many a strange and unexpected experience, during the war and since, but the climb to the top of those cliffs was one of the strangest.

The only way to the top was by way of a set of crude steps, cut in the solid rock, up the sheer rock face. We found the first steps and started to climb; no guard rails; no lights. It was the beginning of a climb that none of us would ever forget, as we inched our way upwards, into the impenetrable darkness, not knowing where we were or what lay ahead. In all there were some 300 steps before we finally reached the crest of the rocky cliff, there to stand in total darkness, the shrieking of the wind relieved occasionally by the faint rumble of the loading operations far below. There wasn't a sign of either the iron-ore ships or the Kamsack, even though we knew they lay directly below us.

True adventurers, we set off across the snowy, windblown countryside, following a rough path, which had apparently been trodden by other sailors curious to explore the community of Wabana. There wasn't a house or a person to be seen anywhere. The only sign of life was a flock of sheep, huddled together against the winter blasts. We wondered if we were simply lost, and wandering about in a vast wilderness; but finally, we reached the tiny settlement: a few wooden houses and a general store, whose well-lit interior was a welcome sight after the pitch darkness. The old storekeeper, who had lived all his life on Belle Isle, was delighted to see us, and told us that sailors from the ore ships regularly made their way up the cliff steps and across the wild country to Wabana. He and the other residents of the village were still shocked at the recent sinkings of three ore ships, and the deaths of many merchant sailors whom they had come to know. We spent an hour talking with this old man, bought some tins of seal meat to send home, then set off again to find our way back to the top of the cliffs.

The descent of the 300 steps was even more knee-shaking than the climb, and it was with great relief that we reached the bottom and literally felt our way to the blacked-out Kamsack.

The following morning, in the half-light of a winter dawn, we set off with the three ore ships, now deep in the water with their precious cargoes destined for the waiting steel mills of Sydney. We made our way out of the narrow confines of Conception Bay into the open Atlantic, turned the corner, and set course for Sydney. As the only escort, Kamsack took up her protective station several miles in front of the ships, zig-zagging a screening for the vulnerable vessels.

All was well until late in the day, when, without warning, explosions roared across the water between us and the ore ships: it had to be a U-boat attack on our precious convoy. In minutes, two of the three disappeared from sight, carried to the bottom by the immense weight of their cargoes. As we carried out our frantic search by ASDIC and lookouts searched for the suspected U-boats, we watched in horror as the flickering lights on the life jackets of survivors in the water went out, one by one. It was a terrible ending to a day which had started peacefully at the ore docks in Wabana.

We could make no contact with a U-boat, and finally we were forced to give up and continue with the one surviving ship. We were only able to conclude that the U-boat had made a successful hit-and-run torpedo attack, and was now safely out of range. It was only later that we were told that German mine-laying U-boats had succeeded in laying a string of magnetic mines in our path.

Early in the war, the German navy sent some of their largest U-boats, loaded with magnetic mines, to string deadly mine fields along the entrances to such convoy ports as Halifax and St. John's. Ships like the Kamsack were protected by degaussing gear, which neutralized the magnetism of all-steel ships, but the iron ore ships were completely unprotected from magnetic mines. It was a loss that was to haunt us for weeks to come—and, for some of us, forever—as we struggled against the feeling of helplessness in the face of disaster; the sense of our inadequacy as the protectors of the vulnerable ships. The war had come home to us, there in the darkness near Wabana, Belle Isle.

For me, and for my fellow-sailors, the port of St. John's became a refuge from the cruelties of the war at sea. Our home port was steeped in history: the city, one of the oldest in North America, was founded shortly after John Cabot discovered Newfoundland in 1497. The ties of St. John's to the sea also date back to the fifteenth-century fishing fleets of Britain, Spain, France and Portugal, which fished the riches of the Grand Banks using St. John's as a base from which to operate.

When the Kamsack first entered this landlocked harbour, we had caught sight of some of the famous sailing ships like the Terra Nova—which carried the sealers to the ice floes (and the seals) each spring. There were also ships of many nations in the harbour: corvettes, bangors, destroyers, cruisers, tankers and merchantmen; many of them riddled with gaping holes after attacks by U-boats, which they had miraculously managed to survive. Apart from the ships of the Royal Navy and the Royal Canadian Navy, there were ships of the U.S. Navy, the Free French Navy (including the Surcouf, the world's largest submarine), and even ships from German-occupied Holland, Norway and Poland. The Kamsack became part of this immense concentration of ships and sailors in the strategic seaport of St. John's.

Our usual haunt was the South Side, ringed by hills rising far above the docks where most of the corvettes, bangors and destroyers tied up to provision and prepare for the next encounter. We soon became familiar with the other ships and crews; those we had accompanied or would accompany in escort groups in the months and years ahead. It was with great delight that I would spot an old acquaintance or friend from my training days; from the Montreal draft , Stadacona, or ASDIC school.

Many of us set out on the long hike from the South Side, around the end of the harbour, and into the centre of town. The narrow, cobblestoned streets were jammed with sailors, all searching for a break from life aboard ship. The restaurants were packed with hungry sailors, happy for a rest from everyday fare aboard ship. The movie theatre always had a long lineup. Many a sailor was on the lookout for something to drink other than tea or pop. Beer was often in short supply, but it didn't take long for us to discover the joys of Newfoundland's famous Screech, a liquor based on rum, clear and innocent enough to look at, but powerful enough to knock out even the hardiest of drinkers. Bottles of this native drink passed hands in dark alleys in exchange for a seaman's precious dollars. Well into the night, sailors crawled back on board after polishing off a bottle of Screech. More important than food, drink and movies was a bit of female companionship, for which we sailors were constantly on the lookout. The search often proved to be a tricky business, since sailors vastly outnumbered the girls. There were crowds of seamen pouring ashore; there were soldiers and airmen; and there were our greatest rivals, the Yanks from Fort Pepperall and the American ships. Despite the competition, many a Canadian sailor found romance. Many of them married into St. John's families.

Many of us headed for the hostels which had sprung up with the war, most particularly the Y.M.C.A., the Sally Ann (Salvation Army) and the K of C (Knights of Columbus). In these hostels we found a bed for the night; three-tiered bunks, stacked inches apart in the huge dormitories which reminded me of the Stadacona barracks, except that the beds were real ones! With overnight leave until 0700 hours, it was possible to get a good night's rest, and have supper and breakfast in somewhat more civilized surroundings than the seaman's mess. It was with great sorrow that we heard, much later, of a fire which destroyed the K of C hostel, taking the lives of more than 100 sailors who, like us, had only been looking for a comfortable place to spend a night ashore.

As the Kamsack docked frequently in St. John's, I took to wandering through and around this seaport city, summer and winter, exploring every foot of Bowering Park, revelling in the hike to the top of Cabot Hill and, overlooking the narrow opening to St. John's Harbour, gazing at the famous tower from which Marconi received his historic first radio transmission from a station in Cornwall, England. There were always shrieking gales atop Cabot Hill, strong enough to sweep one off one's feet. There was the wild Atlantic far below. Next stop Ireland. Sometimes, I would continue along the coast, out of St. John's, covering mile after mile on the rugged high cliffs, with the winter seas crashing mightily against the shore far below.

These lonely walks were a great release after life aboard ship. and later, when I made my way back to St. John's, I was tired and hungry. But I always felt better about myself and what was happening to me.

Some evenings, I went to the Caribou Hut, a sailor's refuge where we could sit and write letters, find some books to read, and strike up conversations with Royal Navy sailors and merchant sailors from the many ships in port. I got to know a merchant sailor off the Irish Minstrel who often invited me back on board his ship to meet his fellow crewmen. Later, I made a point of looking for the Irish Minstrel in our convoys, and often wondered if she and her fine crew made it safely through the war. I still don't know—but I hope they did!

But spots like the Caribou Hut and the hostels were no match for the officers' hangout, the Crowsnest, a posh exclusive club where officers could eat, drink, dance with their lady-friends, and generally have a good time. We commoners also had our exclusive pleasures. Since the food situation on board left much to be desired, especially as our runs stretched into weeks, and supplies got scarcer and scarcer, a few of us decided to spend some of our hard-earned seaman's dollars (thirty bucks or so, to begin with) on extra food to carry with us. Ron Cosburn and I were the first to squirrel away some extras: we searched out stores where we could get canned soups, meats and spaghetti, lugged our precious box aboard, and stowed it safely in our ASDIC compartment, under lock and key (theft was not unknown aboard ship). We took quite a ribbing from our fellow crewmen at first:

"Whatcha tryin' to do, Curry, open a grocery?" but they soon picked up the practice themselves.

One of the stores we frequented, far up the hill above St. John's, was run by a kindly gentleman who began saving us copies of Time Magazine, very difficult to find in wartime. One time, when we walked in after many weeks absence, he got quite philosophical, telling us that he envied our young lives and experiences, despite the ever-present dangers. A native of St. John's, he had made a fortune when he was young, and each year afterwards, had promised himself a trip around the world. But before he could take the trip, he lost everything he had in the Great Depression, and never again was able to raise the money to travel.

"I have never been out of the sight of these hills," he said, sadly.

The story made a profound impression on us, and we always made a point of visiting him each time we tied up in St. John's.

St. John's. The city came to enjoy a very special place in our lives. Over the five years which were to follow, we would happily head into the narrow harbour for a welcome rest from the war at sea.

Sea, Ship And Man

Greek ship torpedoed on the far side of the convoy. H.M.C.S. Rimouski picked up some survivors. I split my knee wide open going to Action Stations when I skidded on the icy decks...depth charges going off all around the convoy; turbulent waters, icy mountainous seas...German air activity in the Irish Sea and we came up on it with a Red Warning. Shawinigan dropped back to try and save a lagger...sighted large mass of wreckage and came up on two machine gun-riddled boats; two dead merchant seamen in one; terrible sight... Action Stations at noon; Rimouski at it hot and heavy with sub contact. Our number almost came up; came within inches of being cut in two and sent to the bottom by Greek ship which left the convoy early and came right at us in the pitch dark.

Alongside HMCS Barrie: a gunner put three slugs into his leg; despite every effort to save his life, he bled to death before our very eyes. Terrible time holding onto the convoy during the night. We are taking an awful beating. Two feet of stinking sea water sloshing around in our mess deck; bridge awash, seas breaking over the ship. No dishes left, eating out of empty jam tins; no hot food, impossible for the cooks to keep anything on the galley stoves. Constant reports of German U-boats in our immediate vicinity...dropped two 8-depth charge patterns on solid sub echo; uncertain results. Spotted German long-distance Dornier patrol aircraft lurking just out of

reach on the horizon, no doubt sending back constant reports of our movements...British aircraft attacked surfaced U-boat 150 miles directly ahead of our convoy course...Action Stations at 0930 as Trillium reported sub contact; Action Stations for nine hours straight; constant roar of exploding depth charges.

Set off alone to escort Loch Ewe section of our large convoy...picked up Belfast section of our westward-bound convoy, 76 ships and escort of five corvettes. Action Stations at 2400, picked up sub contact, let go patterns of depth charges...Eyebright came tearing up in pitch black, same contact; between us, we dropped forty charges. Eyebright let go with four-inch shells which whined just over our mast; other side of the convoy broke into turmoil; ocean a mass of exploding depth charges...0900 and still pitch dark; we picked up what seemed to be a surfaced sub in thick fog, 1000 yards off our port bow. We could not get a bead on it but seem to have shaken it off our convoy. W/T picked up nine different German U-boats calling each other and seeming to close in on us. Looks as if we are getting lined up by a wolf pack...all we can do is hold fast to our tight screen and pray none gets into our convoy. W/T still getting fixes on the pack, but we seem to be keeping them out of the convoy...wonderful sight of three American destroyers which bore down on us from Iceland and joined our tight screen. Dirty weather helping: Rain, hail, sunshine and snow, all within the last few hours...terrific winds of hurricane force out of the north; we are being pounded unmercifully...stretched to the breaking point...Relieving escort! What a wonderful sight!

Sharp alteration of course on emergency signal; six to eight German U-boats in pack formation, laying across our course, 300 miles ahead. Flocks of messages pouring in from Convoy W-8 under heavy attack to our north; they lost six ships last night and still under heavy attack. Out of nowhere, we ran into trouble; picked up a sub contact, gave it three patterns...Skeena and Eyebright busy on the other side of the convoy, attacking a single contact...Large convoy ahead of us, escorted by U.S. Navy, under terrible attack...We were detached from our convoy and detailed to go to its aid at all possible speed...took awful beating in mountainous head-on seas...terrible night, never to be forgotten, all-out effort to reach convoy under attack; it had lost sixteen *ships. We took up screening position...Our convoy now ringed tight with extra escorts and looks like we have saved the rest of the convoy from destruction...We lost ship on the far side of the convoy during the night; nothing we could do about it; terrible feeling of helplessness.*

Cosburn picked up a sub contact at 0220, we spent two hours attacking...dropped five full patterns of charges, in pitch dark of storm-ridden night. Found our new convoy; it had lost four ships. Rimouski spotted a sub on the surface... sub's W/T messages fading out. RCAF Coastal Command aircraft attacked a surfaced sub in our vicinity...American planes spotted life raft off our port bow; it was off S.S. McComb, Standard Oil tanker sunk in this vicinity several days ago... Three dead men huddled in life raft.

Large U.S. blimp took up patrol ahead of our convoy, plus dozen U.S. planes... Queen Mary, Queen Elizabeth, Louis Pasteur and Mauretania, four of twelve troop transports in outbound convoy. Tied up just ahead of the HMCS Assiniboine just in from battle with surfaced U-boat off Newfie; sunk it but it caught numerous hits from sub's gunfire. Flock of messages from convoy immediately behind; several ships sunk; found ourselves in trouble; Polish destroyer ahead of us found sub on surface, lying in wait, smashed it open. Rockets being fired in middle of convoy by merchantmen, surfaced subs around. Two large tankers torpedoed. We picked up a contact dead ahead in pitch dark before dawn; we swear we scraped right down its length as it dove to safety; full pattern of charges, uncertain results. Convoy attacked off Sable Island; news of sinking of the HMCS Ottawa; many buddies on board her...I picked up a sub contact at midnight, five attacks on it...Black week for our fellow-RCN ships, now with sinking of HMCS St. Croix with only one lone survivor out of a crew of 200...gives us an awful feeling...

Re-reading my daily diary record, the sparse, abrupt entries jotted down despite conditions which made it almost impossible to record anything at all, I am stunned; and the fear and horror of the war comes flooding back.

It is hard to imagine how any of us could have survived, as ill-prepared as we were for the role of protecting convoys of vulnerable merchantmen;

bringing them home safely, and ensuring that the vital war supplies they carried were able to reach their destinations. How often we came face-to-face with veteran, highly-skilled U-boat commanders. Rank amateurs versus professionals! How often we were led astray; lured away from the convoy or out of ASDIC contact. Perhaps it's just as well that we didn't recognize how weak we were; that we carried on, despite our shortcomings.

We did provide some measure of protection for our all-important merchant ships. Herding them along, screening, probing, investigating, zig-zagging, closing up, lengthening out, doing all we could to keep the U-boats away from the columns of merchantmen. We did drop back to help some ancient freighter, its engines failing, and somehow keep it with the convoy. Time and again, we muddled through, attacking submerged U-boats, driving off a faint shadow on the surface in the pitch dark, holding ASDIC contact and throwing pattern after pattern of depth charges at our unseen but not unheard enemy.

Inevitably we lost contact. Inevitably we were left unsure whether we had succeeded in destroying or even damaging the attacker. But we always tried to stick to the cardinal rules: protect the convoy; save the convoy from attack, never leave the convoy open to U-boats.

Day by day, we gained in knowledge and experience. We had served our apprenticeship. We had brushed up against the war at sea, taken on the full fury of the North Atlantic on the Sydney-Newfie run, developed from rank amateurs into a ship and crew. We would have benefited from practice, but the need was desperate. We were thrown into full-scale battle at a time when the war effort had fallen to its lowest ebb: 1941-42.

Convoy after convoy was being mauled and battered, with so many ships sunk that Churchill felt the war might be lost in the Atlantic. The Germans were adding to their U-boat fleet. Many of their most experienced U-boat commanders were still active. Using their Atlantic bases on the French coast, and adopting highly sophisticated tactics, including attacks by "wolf packs" of as many as eight to ten U-boats, they were able to close in on a convoy, especially with long-distance Dornier aircraft scouting the Atlantic for their prey.

Our convoys were not only under constant attack, but also pitifully short of protection. The limited number of British and Canadian destroyers were being driven beyond the limits of endurance. Gradually, they were getting the help they needed. Increasing numbers of corvettes poured out of the shipyards, received their fledgling crews, and joined the fray. H.M.C.S. Kamsack was one of these. Through sheer necessity, the Kamsack advanced to the Mid-Ocean Group. She was responsible for taking over the eastbound convoys far off Cape Race, Newfoundland, and escorting them through the vast reaches of the mid-Atlantic, on to Iceland, northern Scotland, and the Irish Sea, through the gauntlet of the German U-boat fleet. These convoys were endurance tests for ships and crew alike. Fast convoys, perhaps composed of fast tankers, might take ten to twelve days. Slower convoys, often consisting of seventy to eighty ships, the slowest moving at seven knots an hour, took fourteen to sixteen days; up to twenty-two days during mid-winter storms.

Nothing had prepared us for the hardships of the Mid-Ocean Group. How could we have conceived of the endless death and destruction, the extreme misery, the despair and hopelessness which were to be hammered into our lives as we took on the war at sea at its worst? Still, we wouldn't be alone. We were joining forces with veterans: the River Class destroyers, H.M.C.S. St. Laurent, Assiniboine and Ottawa; newly-acquired four-funnelers of the U.S. Navy, H.M.C.S. Columbia and Annapolis; and the scarred and battered Royal Navy destroyers, H.M.S. Vanoc, Veteran and Burnham. To these were added the Flower Class corvettes, H.M.C.S.

Trillium, Eyebright, Rimouski, Napanee, Battleford, Chambly, Sorel, Oakville, Algoma, Hespeler, Moose Jaw, Barrie, Midland, Agassiz, Bouctouche, Shawinigan and Kamsack. Our escort groups were sometimes led by two River Class destroyers with three corvettes on the sides and rear. When the corvette crews had gained strength and experience, we would reach the point at which five corvettes could assume full responsibility for a seventy-ship convoy.

Our destination? Far up the northwest coast of Scotland to the lonely entrance to Loch Ewe. Somewhere off the southwest coast of Iceland. Down the Irish Sea for the last leg into Liverpool. These were our waters.

The convoys were of every size, shape and speed. After leaving Boston, New York, Baltimore and other U.S. ports, the ships formed up in the vast reaches of Bedford Basin, far up the inner part of Halifax harbour:

there, the captains planned the treacherous Atlantic crossings, giving special attention to the mid-ocean area, far from the protection of land-based aircraft. The convoys were always led by an old master of the seas; often a retired Royal Navy admiral, who would take full control of the convoy from his post on one of the merchant ships, after meeting with the merchant-ship captains to plan strategy and tactics for the long haul ahead. These meetings must have been demanding: the ships hailed from many nations, and were a vast range of vessel sizes, speeds and ages. They were supposed to function as a single unit.

Our departures became a familiar sight to the people of Halifax. Ship after ship left the confines of Bedford Basin and headed down the long stretches of Halifax harbour. Some were majestic and proud, some rusty and battered-looking; each carried a four-inch naval gun, mounted on the afterdeck and manned by a naval gunner's crew, known as DEMS (Defensive Equipment of Merchant Ships). At the same time, the designated escort group slipped out of Halifax, taking up a screening position as the ships formed in pre-arranged columns, their escorts positioned front, sides and aft. The most vulnerable ships, loaded down with ammunition and explosives, and the tankers, were hidden as deeply as possible in the middle of the convoy, with the outer columns made up of stronger, well-armed ships. At front and centre was the ship bearing the convoy master, ready to take charge of direction, movements and alterations of course. The convoy was now ready to set off on its predetermined course, usually for its first rendezvous far off Cape Race, where it would be taken over by the mid-ocean escort group.

Convoys were generally made up of ships of about the same speed, although there was some variation. The six-knot convoys were the slowest and toughest of all, composed of ancient ships which in peacetime would have gone to the scrap heap. Often, their protesting engines broke down at sea, and then came pleading signals to the escort group:

"Engine trouble! Can you stand by me?"

This message forced us into a dreadful dilemma: to leave a vital gap in the protective ring of the convoy, or to leave the stricken ship to the mercy of some trailing U-boat. In daylight, the escort commander would order one ship to drop back, and we would try our best to stay with the lagging ship. But more often, we were forced to break off and abandon the ship to her fate, knowing that her chances of survival were slim. Sometimes, the crew managed to make temporary repairs and rejoin the convoy, but, sadly, many a ship went to the bottom in these circumstances.

Most convoys were composed of nine or ten-knot ships flying the British, Dutch, French, Greek, Norwegian, American and Canadian ("Red Duster") merchant flags. Outward-bound, they were deep in the water with all the materials of war; their decks crammed with bombers, tanks and carriers. Scattered through the inner convoy were the most vulnerable of all—the tankers, some carrying crude oil, many with high-octane aviation fuel. We corvette sailors stood in awe of the merchant sailors who rode the tankers and somehow survived a fiery sinking to return a second, third and even a fourth time, aboard other fuel-laden tankers, to face ever-mounting odds. The all-tanker groups were (apart from the great passenger liners) the fastest of all the convoys, capable of sixteen to eighteen knots, and more. On one occasion, the Kamsack was part of an escort group responsible for twenty such tankers, which were empty and high out of the water, homeward bound from Britain. Compared to a six-knot convoy, this group of tankers tore through the seas, and the Kamsack, with her all-out maximum speed of just under eighteen knots, shook like a motor out of control. We had a terrible time screening, carrying out zig-zag patterns, trying to keep up.

Through the seemingly endless years of sea warfare, the convoys encountered every kind of danger, disaster, and tragedy. A convoy would sail on unmolested, day after day, night after night, weeks on end, with never a sign of trouble. Then, without warning, the terrible deep rumble of a torpedoed ship would reach up from the far side of the convoy, and we would be under attack. The terrifying message, "Action Stations!" would resound throughout the ship, and we would race frantically to our stations. Long-range Dornier patrol aircraft from bases on the French coast would appear over the mid-Atlantic and lurk on the horizon, out of range of our guns. They would be sending back reports on our convoy and directing German

U-boats to our position. (We did have the odd merchant ship equipped with a catapult and a Hurricane fighter, which could be put into a once-only flight to combat German aircraft. The pilot would have to take his chances in the ocean afterwards.)

On other occasions, we would pick up a contact with a U-boat and tear in on it with our attack procedures, dropping pattern after pattern of depth charges, some with shallow (fifty-foot) settings, which almost ripped our own ship apart. Our first aim was to protect. We hoped to discourage, drive off, damage or even destroy the attacker, but the priority was preventing the enemy from penetrating the convoy. Sometimes, the attacks would go on for hours; sometimes, contact would be lost; sometimes, the U-boat commanders would unload a mess of oil, lifejackets and clothing to give us a false sense of security and shake us off the trail. Sometimes, our wireless operators would pick up the conversations of half-a-dozen U-boats, closing in for a mass attack on our convoy, and we would be caught in a hopeless situation; sometimes, we would be attacking invisible foes, hidden in the depths and only accessible through ASDIC. During these bouts of blind warfare, both sides resorted to every trick in the book, and we corvette sailors learned fast, quickly becoming more experienced, and more cunning.

On one occasion, as we made our way out of the Irish Sea into the open Atlantic, homeward bound with a large convoy of seventy ships, we began to pick up messages from another westbound convoy some two days ahead of us, under heavy attack by a pack of U-boats. A number of ships had already been lost by the time the desperate calls for help went out from the escort leader. As the closest convoy, ours received the call, and the Kamsack was detached to go to the aid of the stricken convoy. Even at all-out speed, pounding and rattling and plunging through the heavy seas of the mid-Atlantic, it took what seemed like years to reach the convoy, which was still under attack. Finally, we located it, widely scattered but managing to keep some semblance of positions and columns. The U-boat pack was still hanging on for further attacks, but, as time passed, the increased protection from the Kamsack and several other ships which had been detached from their convoys seemed to turn the tide, and the attacks ceased. But a dozen merchantmen were torpedoed, and sunk.

Not all torpedoed ships would sink, and the North Atlantic waters were often full of ships with as many as four gaping torpedo holes in their sides; ships with their bows torn off; even oil tankers, which, despite the great gashes in their sides, did not catch fire or sink, especially if they had divided tanks. Every port, on both sides of the Atlantic, had its share of torpedoed ships which managed to make it to port, where they were repaired to sail another day. Most of these crippled ships made it under their own power; others were pulled to safety by powerful, armed, sea-going tugs which ranged the oceans and risked being sunk themselves while helping wounded ships.

As the war went on, defences against U-boats improved. We started out with the benefit of ASDIC; we continued with an even more effective innovation: radar. This technology turned night into day for us (although, in the early days of radar, the operators often kept the set going by kicking and cursing it). By the end of the war, convoys were escorted by a vastly improved version of the corvette, the frigate, and attack groups ranged far ahead of the convoy to seek out and destroy U-boats headed for the convoy. (The most outstanding example was Captain Walker and his Royal Navy sloops, which were deadly in locating and destroying U-boats lying in wait for an approaching convoy.) As well, Coastal Command aircraft increasingly roamed the Atlantic and attacked surfaced U-boats.

A perennial problem in escorting a convoy was that merchantmen had their own idiosyncracies, the most troublesome being a tendency to separate from the convoy to proceed to port. Such manoeuvres were always pre-arranged, but there was always one ship which left an hour before the scheduled departure time. On more than one occasion, we were almost cut in two by a merchantman coming out of the dark and bearing down on us.

"Ship bearing red 020!" came the lookout's frightened voice, and the captain quickly gave the order to alter the course full away. At those moments, we felt as if our world were coming to an end, as the two ships slid down each other's sides in the darkness, with inches separating them.

There are a thousand memories of the great convoys, some 100 ships strong; spread out over a vast patch of ocean; almost lost in terrible winter storms; and, under attack, scattered and thrown to the winds, sometimes never to re-group. There are memories of freezing winter nights and sudden calls to Action Stations; of flares, and explosions and disaster in the convoy; of bullet-ridden sea boats and life rafts, laden with their dead, floating in the empty vastness of the North Atlantic; of fellow corvettes torpedoed, and lost with all hands.

Sometimes, the convoy experience was weird; strange; unbelievable. The Kamsack once escorted a convoy for eight solid days in a fog that never lifted for an instant. During those eight days, we never once caught a glimpse of the thirty ships we were escorting, and when we turned them over to another escort, we picked up an incoming convoy, equally invisible in the still-heavy fog. Once again, we escorted the convoy, this one of twenty ships—for another eight days, still beset by impenetrable fog. The ships were there, with their crews, a stone's throw away, but nary a sight of ship nor man. Sixteen days in all, with some fifty ships, and never a glimpse of our flock. Such were the vagaries of sea and ship and man.

Curiously, the most vulnerable, and, at the same time, most unconquerable, were the young, untried sailors who shared life on a small ship for weeks at a time, facing the dangers, the tragedies, and the sorrows of war. Young and resilient as we were, there were times each of us felt we could not go on. I vividly recall occasions on which I was certain that I could face it all no longer; that I had to give in, simply let myself slip over the side in the darkness, into the all-encompassing Atlantic, for I no longer had the will to continue. I don't know where I found the strength to resist this urge; to push myself back from the breaking point. Perhaps many fellow-sailors who were "lost at sea" were, in fact, victims of the same breakdown which plagued us all; but they, tragically, succumbed to the sea's dark seductive pull.

The pressure got to us all in some way. I soon began to dread leaving port; taking on yet another convoy; facing another solo ASDIC watch: two hours on, four hours off, day and night; solely responsible for safeguarding the ship, my 125 shipmates, and the whole wing of the convoy. It sounds self-serving—to say that everyone depended on my ability to fulfil my role—but there was nothing conceited about being deadly tired and deathly ill, vomiting and retching into the bucket wedged against the ASDIC set, and going on, twenty-four hours a day, three or more weeks into eternity. In the grim night watches, fully clothed and wrapped in my high-slung hammock for four short hours of respite before the next watch, I was often unable to sleep for fear of the dreaded thump on my hammock from the quartermaster, warning me that I was due back on watch in fifteen minutes. And then it all began again. I slid out of the hammock to the steel deck, awash with sea water (and worse). Still bone-tired, half-sick, clutching at the stanchions as the ship plunged and rolled, I glanced at the weary off-watch sailors wedged, fully clothed as I had been, onto the lockers or in their hammocks, with their lifejackets wrapped around them. Stretching out every precious moment away from the ASDIC, I finally ventured outside, to climb the narrow steps to the bridge, holding on for dear life as the seas crashed over the fo'c'sle and pounded against the ship. Then, to force open the door of the wheelhouse and feel my way in the darkness to the ASDIC set, as the quartermaster, barely visible in the gloom, fought the wheel to keep on course despite the plunges of the Kamsack. (If I were a moment late, I'd be greeted by a muttered curse from Cosburn, the same way I'd greet a late relief myself) and, late or not, there would be no conversation as he scurried off below, leaving me to my two endless hours of intense and nerve-wracking ASDIC operation.

After an hour or so, a fellow seaman might press a cup of scalding hot kye into my hand, growling,

"Try this on for size."

It was a relief, as I sat struggling to concentrate, to get the cup of thick, fatty cocoa, lashed with lots of canned milk; despite my turbulent stomach, the brew would stay down and make me feel better for a few moments. If the watch went well, no echoes or disturbances, a thump on my back told me the two hours were up; Telfer was ready to relieve me.

In the first months of the Kamsack's operations, we were sadly lacking in winter clothing. It was a sorry sight to see the men forced to strip off ice-coated, threadbare duffel coats, and turn them over to those going on watch. We were ill-equipped to face the North Atlantic's winter seas and storms, and it would be a long wait for adequate clothing. Much later we received the well-designed "zoot suits," which were warmly lined, waterproof, and zipped up from head to toe. What's more, there was one per sailor. As well, there were full lifejackets, equipped with flashing rescue lights, a far cry from the old "Mae West" blow-ups, which were useless.

Not that my inadequate clothing was foremost in my mind as I made my way below after my watch. Sleep was the top priority. Some men collapsed on the lockers which had just been vacated; others, like me, crawled into their hammocks, wet and miserable, to sleep the sleep of the weary. A few of the hardier souls among us grabbed a loaf of bread, often mouldy, and hacked off thick slabs to make huge onion sandwiches. These gave off an unbelievable stench to those unfortunate enough to have slung their hammocks over the mess tables. And just as the mess deck settled into sleep, we were likely to be torn awake by shrill, pulsating alarm bells; the call to Action Stations; and a mad, scrambling dash as we raced through the pitch dark to our stations. More often than not, ASDIC had reported a suspicious echo, and no chances were taken in bringing the ship to readiness.

There was a long and agonizing wait: was this the beginning of some dreadful attack? The order would usually be:

"Secure. Return to regular watches."

"Those bloody ping-happy ASDICs!" some sailors would mutter. Sometimes, it was the real thing, starting with the terrifying rumble of a torpedo striking one of our merchantmen. Then, the call to Action Stations would mean hours and hours of devastating and tragic events: ships ripped apart; ship's crews killed; ASDIC contacts lost, regained, lost forever; pattern after pattern of depth charges; the darkness briefly illuminated by star shells; our ship manoeuvering on attack orders, veering and turning to keep contact with the enemy; the crew fearfully trying to do all that was required in these times of supreme challenge.

In the years of the war at sea, we became accustomed to spending all night fending off the enemy, with relief only coming with the dawn. In the most protracted struggles, when several ships could be lost during attacks which lasted for days, there would be periods when we never left our closed-up positions. During times like these, all our youthful bravado deserted us; we were overwhelmed by events beyond our control; by odds which were so often stacked against us; by a highly skilled and effective enemy. But we gained experience, bitterly-won experience, and became more proficient in bringing convoys safely home to Britain or North America without loss.

It was like entering paradise when the Kamsack finally made port.

What a pleasure it was to get away from the ship, even to Britain's wartime ports, cruelly battered and almost destroyed by German bombers, and feel the solid ground beneath our feet again! Perhaps it was knowing that we would return to the war at sea again in a matter of days that made shore leave so precious: the warmth of English pubs, the mugs of bitters, the human companionship, the wet canteen, the public house, the bootlegger in a dark alley, the girls, the dance halls or on the streets of any port.

Sometimes, the release we sought was no more complicated than a soccer game. With our ship tied up for a few hours, and no shore leave, the crew got hold of a soccer ball and turned the jetty into a field, for the wildest game. It was a no-holds-barred soccer, with plenty of kicking and butting, as we released every pent-up feeling, battered each other into bruised submission, and finally climbed back aboard to collapse, exhausted yet restored. In some ports, we managed to gain access to a gymnasium, where we had a two-hour game of floor hockey, a game which must be the most savage sport ever invented, especially the way we played it. But the vio-

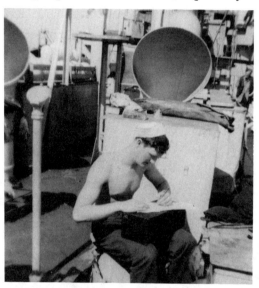

lent exercise did a lot to relieve the miseries buried deep within us. Others settled for a good meal, a haircut, a night in a hostel bed, a hot shower, and a long walk in the English and Irish countryside—another effective way to restore the soul; to try to ready oneself for the return to the war at sea.

As for me, there was the strange need to recall what was happening to us all; to keep my strictly-forbidden diary, which, when discovered by my shipmates, became a source of endless jokes at my expense. I think they were both puzzled and suspicious about my desire to write about our experiences. Wasn't it bad enough to have to go through it all without re-living it again on paper? I'm sure that more than a few of them thought I was a little odd. But despite the many reasons for letting it go, I spent five long years jotting down the feelings, the events, the exhilaration, the fury of war, and the magic of the hours of respite.

Sometimes, the release came in a good old-fashioned brawl. Sailors clashed with each other or with civilians; shop windows were smashed; and patrols lugged bleeding and drunken sailors back to their ships, or to lock-up. One of the Kamsack's crew members, a small wiry Cape Bretoner, took great delight in importing Glace Bay's favourite form of Saturday-night entertainment: a full-scale brawl in the main street. His closest chum on board was a French-Canadian who had drifted to the textile mills of Fall River, Massachusetts. Together, they were a formidable twosome who liked nothing better than to find, or start, a brawl ashore, and unleash their fighting talents in the fray. Such an occasion presented itself one time in the lovely old town of Lunenburg, Nova Scotia, where the good people had arranged a dance for our war-weary crew while our ship was tied up for a refit. The dance was a great success until the evening began to wind down, and the consumption of liquor escalated at such a rate that half the crew took to the streets and battled amongst themselves in a wild, terrifying night of blood, battered faces, broken noses and black eyes. It was as if all the years of harsh and brutal living conditions had finally turned us into animals, who revelled at being able to hack each other into submission.

Often, through the long years of despair, our pent-up feelings found temporary release in man's oldest source of comfort—alcohol; in our case, the demon rum. Although the daily rum ration was supposed to be consumed as issued, and was often mixed with water, most crews seemed to get around the rules, and vast quantities of 120-per-cent over-proof rum were stored throughout the ship in crew's lockers.

Much was carried ashore and consumed there, or sold; but enough remained on board to provide the basis for periodic breakouts, and they were wild. It was always a startling experience to return from shore leave to find a good part of the crew roary-eyed drunk and in a vile mood, the ship in a turmoil. Who could blame them? The breaking point was often very close for crews who had faced weeks and months of filth, cold and hunger, and all the worst conditions of winter seas on small ships, only to have insult added to injury.

There was one time when the ship was about to go into drydock, and the crew was looking forward to a long-anticipated (and well-deserved) leave. The incident began with a junior officer reporting a clock stolen from his cabin. All the sailors' lockers, but none of the officers' cabins, were searched; then, the captain announced that if the clock was not returned by noon, all leaves would be cancelled. The crew was in a vile mood, and when the clock showed up, hours later, in the possession of another officer—he had forgotten all about borrowing it—the ship was close to the breaking point, and the rum came out of all the hiding places to turn the crew into a wild, almost mutinous mass of infuriated men.

Such occurrences were not rare. In the English Channel, after weeks and weeks of slogging, no sign of shore leave, and misery piling upon misery, the crew found it a little hard to take when fresh bread was carried on board to the officers' wardroom, and we were left with the mouldy, hard remnants which passed as bread for the lower deck. Once again, we would come close to cracking under the pressure of our resentment; and the hard-saved bottles of pusser rum were broken out on the double.

Sadly, some of our crew gave way to their frustrations by jumping ship for a few brief hours of freedom when we were in port but not on shore leave. Then came the ultimate humiliation: a ship's court-martial on the quarterdeck; the tearing off of the poor sailor's hatband, badges and naval collar. He was left standing there completely stripped of his identity as a sailor in Her Majesty's Canadian Navy; and the charges were read out. There was no trial: he was simply sentenced and taken ashore in handcuffs, between two of his shipmates, armed with rifles and bayonets. The rest of us, who hadn't had the same nerve, nevertheless empathized with our shipmate's humiliation; we knew very well that these shows of power represented the navy's way of keeping us all in line.

Later, the blow-ups among frustrated sailors took on even stranger dimensions. One night, we were tied up in Plymouth with no shore leave. The mood was ugly, and our tight-knit little society was steadily deteriorating, as our resentment built against the damage that the war was doing to our lives. The talk grew bitter and dangerous; tempers flared; before long, the ship was in total bedlam as the private supplies of rum appeared and any veneer of civilization vanished. All over the ship, there was fighting, cursing, arguing and spewing. It was degrading and depressing; an awful reflection on us and our lives. The war and what it had done to us. At the end of the horrible night, someone broke into the sailors' canteen, took all our precious stores of duty-free Canadian cigarettes, scooped them out of their cartons, and very deliberately scattered them through a porthole onto the surface of the harbour. Next morning, thousands of cigarettes, floating and bobbing in the gentle swell, met the astonished gaze of the early watch. They seemed a grotesque metaphor for the emptiness and meaninglessness we all felt.

On The Derry Run

Until shortly before the Kamsack was attached to the St. John's "Newfie" base as part of the Mid-Ocean Group, the usual pattern of convoy movement was to pick up the eastbound convoy somewhere off Cape Race on the southeasterly tip of Newfoundland, then head towards Iceland. Somewhere off Iceland, the escorts would hand over the convoy to a British group and head into Reykjavic to refuel, provision and pick up a westbound convoy. As usual, we, the lowly crew, weren't officially told of any plan to change this itinerary, but rumours were that our next convoy would end up in the new Canadian naval base in Londonderry, Northern Ireland. The rumour mill was right on target: when next we headed out through "The Hole in the Wall," in company with the destroyers Assiniboine and Restigouche, and our fellow corvettes Eyebright, Shediac and Rimouski, we were indeed bound for Ireland.

But first, the inevitable and wearisome task of loading fresh supplies of food, water, depth charges and ammunition. Often the supplies were moved by hand, over the decks of as many as five ships tied up alongside each other; more than once a greasy depth charge or carrier, a box of bread, or a hunk of slithery beef would slip from the grasp of frozen hands and disappear into the murky water between ships. Day and night, base maintenance gangs would crawl from ship to ship, trying to make sure everything was ready for the next operation. Finally, there was the mail, brought on board just before the lines were cast ashore and we headed for the open seas.

Then, final sailing orders and a last look at our home port, before venturing out into the unknown future. St. John's is a protected harbour, yet not invulnerable to winter gales; our departures, at dawn, were often a breathtaking experience, as we gazed at the clean white blanket of snow on the jetties and the hills towering above us, magnificent and striking. But we didn't leave winter behind, even as we pulled away from the ice and the snowy, rock-bound coast. Stretching at least 150 kilometres to the east was

one vast stretch of pack ice, unbroken and alive with the ceaseless movement of the seas beneath. We opened up narrow lanes—which quickly closed behind us—and the bow smashed into the ice floes with a cacophony created by the smash of the steel hull against the ice. Hour after hour, we hammered our way through the ice, our escort group small dark specks in the white expanse stretching to the horizon. It was as if we had entered another world.

Then, we left the pack ice behind and were back in the familiar winter seas of the North Atlantic: unending northeast gales and heaving cold waves, vast and overpowering. Our ragged line of seventy merchant ships, staggered over many kilometres of ocean, hung together through the brief hours of daylight and the long, danger-filled nights, the storms and the pounding seas. Our escort group of two destroyers and three corvettes kept station, seven to fifteen kilometres off the rim of the convoy, and we ploughed our way eastward, day after day. Sometimes, the relentless head-on gales held us so thoroughly in their grasp that we were unable to make any headway at all, and our noon position one day was exactly as it had been twenty-four hours earlier.

Food was another matter on the long haul to Britain. A few days out of St. John's, we ran out of fresh milk and bread; then, fresh vegetables and meat. The eggs lasted a little longer, but they, too, soon disappeared. The bags of potatoes hung on a bit longer still, but, all too soon, our meals came out of cans. Red lead (canned tomatoes) and bacon was a favourite of the cooks (and the bane of the crew) and salt cod was another. One time, a cook failed to soak the stuff overnight, and almost poisoned the entire crew. It took one of our Newfie crew members to set him straight. When the food supplies petered out, and weather conditions made cooking on the galley stove impossible, the situation really got desperate, and we often had to make do with one tin of sardines and some hardtack as an evening meal. Nor were bully beef and hardtack much of an improvement. We were always hungry, usually seasick, and forever obsessed with the thought of making it to port and getting a square meal.

Word came through that we were to turn our convoy over to a British escort group far up the northwest coast of Scotland, off lonely Loch Ewe, and, after completing the turnover, head for Londonderry—Derry, as it was widely known. Full speed ahead in the winter darkness; then, a magical moment when, long before we had sighted land in the light of dawn, we could smell the precious tang of the earth, somewhere near, the unforgettable sensation shared by all sailors all over the world; the feeling of coming home from the sea. What a moment for our forlorn, weary, beaten, half-starved crew! Then, as the day brightened, there it was: the verdant beauty of Ireland coming up over the horizon. We were safe, we were alive, and at last we were in sight of land, after almost three weeks of winter's torment.

Soon, we were off Moville (Irish Free State) at the entrance to Loch Foyle, and we immediately moved alongside the tanker Scottish Musician to fill our almost-empty fuel tanks. Here occurred one of the most delightful experiences which could ever happen to tired, half-starved sailors:

small boats started to come alongside the Kamsack, and friendly, cheerful Irishmen were soon engaged in bartering dozens of live chickens and baskets of fresh eggs, in exchange for packets of Canadian cigarettes from our canteen. Even the non-smokers soon had handfuls of packets (the going rate was three ten-cent packs of smokes for a live chicken). Soon, most crewmen were clutching the squawking birds and baskets of eggs; all over the ship, sailors were busy wringing the birds' necks, slitting their throats, plucking them, and scattering the feathers to the wind. One of my most treasured photographs, taken with my $1.99 Kodak, is not of sinking a submarine or of "D-Day" landings near Cherbourg, but this one of the crew of the Kamsack wringing the necks of chickens on this, our first encounter with Ireland!

We had the birds ready for cooking in no time: there was a mad rush to the galley, where the cooks did their best to get the dozens of chickens crammed into the small ovens. Other sailors got busy breaking eggs into a pan, a half-dozen at a time, and frying them on a corner of the galley stove. Everywhere, the hungry crew of the Kamsack polished off pans of eggs as they waited for the chickens to finish roasting. Finally, they were ready. No fancy china or silver cutlery needed, we simply took the whole chickens and tore them to pieces, cramming great burning chunks into our mouths. I can't remember anything that ever tasted better.

We were now ready for our first glimpse of Paradise. The Kamsack made its way slowly up garden-like Loch Foyle, passing countless gardens alive with flowers and lush green grass. It was like a dream. The snow and ice of Newfoundland, the winter gales, the heavy grey seas were no more. We were surrounded on both sides with the utter beauty of green Ireland, and it was as if the fairies themselves had wafted us into a land of magic that was almost beyond belief. Loch Foyle was so narrow all the way into Derry that we felt we could almost reach out and touch this beautiful land—peaceful, gentle and lush. It did much to restore our souls, even though we knew we would only have forty-eight hours' layover. For those brief hours and days, we would become human beings again; in touch with peace and beauty and tranquility; far removed from all the ugliness of war. We crept alongside the jetty of the ancient walled city of Londonderry to tie up just below the historic post office. Lines were secured, and engines stopped. We were ready to step ashore; for me, a very special moment, for this was the land of my parents and ancestors. I had returned to my homeland for the first time.

Early in the war, before Canadian ships had started to use Derry as their overseas base, it had never crossed my mind that I might someday start out in search of my parents' Irish ancestors. Not that I hadn't been steeped in the family history of the Currys of Mullaghmeen, Enniskillen in County Fermanagh, and the Whites and Currys of Dublin. But they had always seemed part of a faraway land which I would never see, until the Kamsack landed in Derry to refuel, and provision.

The historic walled city was a welcome respite from the North Atlantic, and was quickly established as a home port, much like St. John's (at the western end of our convoy runs). It didn't take long to establish a routine; first, right outside the dockyard gates, a fish-and-chip shop; nearby, a pub which quickly became a favourite; and a little further, a terrific barbershop, where a chatty Derry barber gave us a good trim for all of a shilling.

Once we had found our bearings in this fine ancient city, many of us would wander far and wide, sometimes climbing the rugged stone wall, which had fended off invaders over the centuries; sometimes walking for miles, circling the city from high above the streets. Then, there were those interested in other scenic wonders, the lovely Derry girls, whom we usually met in hot, stuffy, crowded and lively dance halls.

I shared in all these experiences, but at the same time, my thoughts were dominated by a single driving idea: I must somehow get to my father's ancestral home, however difficult the journey and no matter what the obstacles. I was already used to the vagaries of war, which briefly took the ship to a new and exciting port, only to refuel and set sail again, never to return. This might also be the case in Derry, and the knowledge made me all the more determined to succeed. The captain was deeply sympathetic, and said he wished he could let me go; unfortunately, we were under twenty-four-hours' sailing notice, which meant no official leave, for anyone.

My deep disappointment, which must have shown on my face, seemed to hit a responsive chord: the captain looked at me, hesitated, and finally made an unorthodox decision. The Kamsack would probably not sail for forty-eight hours, he said. If I wanted to take the chance and head out on my own, without a leave permit, risking arrest by a shore patrol or court-martial as a deserter if I missed the sailing, then he would look the other way. I would be entirely on my own.

I didn't hesitate for a moment. In no time, I was ready to leave the ship and head off in search of my father's home. All my shipmates cheered me on, wishing me success in my search and hoping I would make it back to the ship before she sailed. And so I headed into Derry.

But once I had managed to get off the Kamsack, I realized that my knowledge of location was somewhat vague, and related only to the tales of my childhood. I knew that my father had lived on a farm near Enniskillen, which would be my first stop. But it was Sunday, no train, and only a roundabout bus route, which turned out to be halfway around Northern Ireland. At eight in the evening, the bus stopped for an hour in a small country town, where an English army officer and I had the entire dining room to ourselves, and enjoyed a fine dinner in front of a roaring fire. Then, it was back on the bus again, with only two other passengers. After midnight, in a cold, heavy rain, the bus stopped and the driver announced that we had reached Enniskillen.

I was the only remaining passenger, and it was a strange feeling to step off into the winter night, alone in a strange town, with no lights anywhere. I felt hopelessly lost, desperately tired, and unsure what to do next. I felt my way along the deserted and silent street. I sensed I was in front of a hotel, but its iron gates were closed; not a light beckoned; not a sign of life in sight. I groped in the darkness and found what turned out to be the night bell, which I pulled again and again; at last, the doors were thrown open and the night porter appeared, listened to my story, and welcomed me in from the wet and darkness. Soon, he had me tucked away in a room and brought me hot water for a bath.

I awoke to bright sunshine, and started to take in my surroundings. I was in the Imperial Hotel. Much later, I was to learn from my mother that she stayed at the Imperial when she arrived from Dublin to meet my father, just before their wedding! I headed down to the dining room, where I was served a grand Irish breakfast of hot oatmeal porridge with cream, thick bacon with eggs, and mountains of toast: a fine start to my day in and around Enniskillen.

I set out to continue my search for my father's home, and it struck me that the place to start was with the police, the Irish Constabulary. I asked the way and was soon in the local barracks, where I told my tale to a burly sergeant, who listened with keen interest. When he asked me if my Uncle Frank had gone to Canada in the early 1930s and returned to Ireland when the great drought struck Western Canada, I knew I was on the right track. The sergeant called a constable, told him he was to do a special patrol out Mullaghmeen way, and asked him to drop me off at the Curry farm. With a warm farewell, he sent me on my way.

The constable headed off down country lanes, and stopped at a white-washed farmhouse. People started to come from all directions, filled with curiosity, and then, tremendous excitement, for a Curry boy had appeared out of nowhere. After talking to my Uncle Frank, Aunt Lucy and my cousins, I was taken to all the neighbouring farms, including the Dundas farm, home of my paternal grandmother's family, after which Dundas, Ontario, is named. On through the day and far into the night, it was talk, talk talk; and eat, eat, eat. At midnight, exhausted but still keyed up, I tumbled into bed in my father's home. It was a dream come true.

Early the following morning, after a hearty breakfast, my cousin Cecil took me in a horse-drawn buggy to the train station in Enniskillen, where I caught the one train which would get me back to Derry that day. The train had to cross a part of the Irish Free State, and I was told to put my sailor's hat under my coat so as not to give the impression I was a man in uniform travelling through a neutral country. Late that day, I was back in Derry; and I high-tailed it over to the post-office dock. There was the Kamsack, and I breathed a sigh of relief as I crossed the gangway, still keyed up after my adventure.

It would be more than two years before I made my way back to Enniskillen and my father's family; by then, they had given me up for dead (my ship must have sunk) and the welcome they gave me was tremendous.

The Kamsack and her crew soon became veterans on the Derry run from St. John's to Londonderry. Our escort group of five ships, two destroyers and three corvettes, worked its way across the lonely mid-Atlantic with slow convoys of six-knotters, fast groups of tankers, ships flying the flags of many allied nations. The Kamsack and her companion ships H.M.C.S. Saguenay, St. Laurent and Ottawa, and fellow corvettes H.M.C.S. Eyebright, Trillium, Rimouski, Sherbrooke, Oakville and Lethbridge formed many combinations, sometimes joining forces with the juicer destroyers H.M.S. Burnham, Vanoc and Veteran.

In one bag of mail from home, a shipmate received a home-town newspaper containing an article on his wartime experiences on the North Atlantic convoys. After glowing tributes to his role in getting the convoys safely to Britain (he had managed this feat single-handedly, by the sounds of it!) the article went on to say that he was enjoying the work. Now that the sailors were getting ample bundles of woollen mitts and scarves from home, it continued, winter in the North Atlantic wasn't really all that bad.

"Little do they know," our shipmate's expression said it all as he showed us the article.

We all silently agreed, as the Kamsack prepared to leave St. John's with a convoy of eighty-six ships bound for Britain. The security of a ship tied to the jetty, motionless and quiet, was behind us; the luxury of fresh water from shore, and hot showers, was gone. No more mail; no more nights ashore, in a bed; no more clean and dry clothes; no more regular meals, although some of us invested a portion of our wartime pay (thirty-one dollars a month plus board) in boxes to tuck away for lean days ahead.

The crew was silent as the Kamsack cleared the gates, and plunged into the grey and frigid seas. Our minds were full of apprehension as we contemplated another three weeks of misery, uncertainty and danger. As our convoy made its way across the vast emptiness of the mid-Atlantic, the ceaseless northeasterly gales took total possession of our lives. The great rolling waves came directly at us, day and night. Our eighty-six ships, spread out in columns over a huge patch of ocean, disappeared completely from sight, masts and all, as the Kamsack rode the crest of one massive wave and rolled down it as if on a roller-coaster's first steep plunge. Sometimes, we caught glimpses of our fellow corvettes, waves breaking over them as they, too, dug their bows into the depths and reared up to face the next wave. It was overwhelming. We were so small and insignificant in the clutches of the elements.

Life on board dragged on, hour by hour, day into night, night into day. Our spirits were already at a low ebb, and as conditions grew worse, we began, again, to feel as if we were living like animals. The water made its way into the mess decks, as it always did. It seemed the whole ocean was swirling inside the ship—a sensation to which none of us, no matter how hardened, ever grew accustomed. Like the ocean, the mess deck contained an unbelievable amount of flotsam and jetsam: seamen's shore-going hats, jam tins, socks, sweaters, and bits of mouldy bread from a loaf which the sea water had finally disintegrated. No wonder it was called a mess deck!

After weeks of this never-ending battering by the seas, we became aware of yet another occupational disease: constant, wrenching pain in our hips. The problem was caused by bracing ourselves against an anticipated blow from a powerful oncoming wave, and while the unnatural posture also affected our knees and legs, it was our hips which took most of the punishment. The pain was a constant companion.

There were periods during which the Atlantic relented, but never for long enough. Winter seemed to last most of the year, bringing northeasterly gales—some of hurricane force—mountainous waves, and cold, dismal days and nights.

One Christmas, the cooks were trying to prepare something hot for the evening meal. the pots were secured by bars on the galley stove but the men had to continually clutch at the stove as the Kamsack reared and slewed in the gale. Suddenly, as we stood in line at the galley entrance, it was as if we were in an elevator which had suddenly plunged out of control from the top of a building. The skylight over the galley was smashed, and torrents of icy sea water poured inside. Pots on the stove were wrenched loose and flew across the galley, their contents flung to the deck. And all our Christmas parcels, which we had considered safely stowed over a ventilator shaft outside the galley, came hurtling down into the mess. Our reaction? Uncontrollable, hysterical laughter. We laughed till we cried, but it was the laughter of desperate men, caught up in the madness of war.

On one convoy, we underwent an experience to which none of us could react with laughter. It was a late winter sailing. The Kamsack, two fellow corvettes, two destroyers and a slow convoy of eighty merchant ships were bound for Britain. As soon as we had cleared the narrows of St. John's and met the first waves, we knew this would be a rough passage. But there was no turning back. The convoy grouped, the previous escort turned back to the home port, and we pointed our bow east. Almost immediately, the Kamsack was full of water; the mess decks were awash; dishes were tumbling and smashing to the deck; all sorts of supposedly secure items were breaking loose and floating freely around in the muck. Life was back to normal in the North Atlantic.

But the abnormal set in. The great northeasterly gales grew in force, and we began to realize that we were in the grip of something far beyond our previous experiences with winter gales; something mighty, awesome, and fearful to behold. The winds grew in intensity to reach Force Twelve , hurricane force, and maintained levels of 100 kilometres per hour, for days. It seemed unbelievable that winds of this power could go on, and on, but they did. Yet, despite the devastating effects of the gale, its might was majestic. And it had to be admired as a tyrannical god is admired. The sustained shrieking through the ship's rigging; the visible results of its power, the relentless surge from the ever-grey seas; this was all part of the true

power of nature, beside which we humans paled into puniness and insig-
nificance. The seas mounted so high that our ships seemed to be nothing
more than wood-chips on a vast ocean. The 1200-ton Kamsack climbed
one mighty wave after another, sometimes caught at the peak and buried
deep under its crumbling crest; sometimes reaching the summit only to
slide into the terrifying trough between two waves, as if to plunge to the
bottom of the sea. Everything disappeared from sight, and there were only
waves, towering far above us, on all sides. And then we would climb to
the next onslaught of water. We were often completely out of sight of the
rest of the convoy, as ships like us slid into the depths; then, for an instant,
we would catch a glimpse of a mast before we plunged out of sight once
more. These occurrences weren't new to us; but what was a first was the
duration. Again and again, I wondered: will one of these huge waves just
bury us and carry us to the bottom? How can we continue to endure these
blows? Yet we did—for days, for weeks; for what seemed an eternity.

Somehow, the convoy held together, although, scattered as it was, it
made slow progress toward Britain. It was to be the longest convoy crossing I had ever experienced. But the Kamsack's fine British trawler design
saw her through in good shape. As always before sailing, we had battened

down everything, and tightened and re-tightened guy wires, lashings, sea
boats, rafts, depth charges—anything that could break loose in such a gale.
Most things held: our port sea boat was torn loose in the rough going, but

we managed to keep it from being washed overboard by lashing it down. Our mess decks were a horrible sight, with sea water, broken dishes, clothes and food swirling around in one foul mess that was with us all the way to Britain.

But other ships in the convoy were less fortunate. One of our fellow corvettes had her entire bridge virtually torn loose from its moorings. On another corvette, a depth charge broke free and started rolling around the ship, crushing a seaman and breaking his leg in several places before one of his shipmates wrestled it to safety.

We all survived, somehow, reaching the northwest coast of Scotland and Loch Ewe; turning over our convoy, without a loss; then heading eagerly toward Derry, and our British base. Never was a return to port more joyous. It was always a fine feeling to reach the shelter of land, and to know that the seas would soon be left behind, if only for a short time. This time, we knew we had faced the ultimate test of the North Atlantic and its winter seas, and had emerged intact. The feeling was a sense of amazement that we had endured.

More Adventures...And A Farewell

There she stood, the rusted, salt-encrusted veteran of the North Atlantic—my ship, the Kamsack. And there I stood, alone in the half-light of dawn, bidding her, and my mates, goodbye.

Leaving a ship which has become your home is one of the saddest experiences in a sailor's life, and one which can never be erased from memory. As I stood there, that day in 1942, saying farewell to my first corvette, I couldn't help recalling just a few other vivid experiences of my years with the Kamsack.

THE WRECK OF THE *AWATEA*

The crew of the Kamsack was chafing at the bit as we neared our home base (Halifax, at the time) after yet another long haul with a convoy. We were almost within sight of the outer reaches of Halifax Harbour; Chebucto Head would soon rise over the horizon; and in a matter of hours, we would be tied up alongside. The bags of mail would land on board, and the crew would scramble into Number One uniforms, ready to go ashore for food, drink, fun and excitement.

But there are no guarantees in war, especially when it comes to shore leave. As we awaited the docking, frantic messages began to pour in from shore stations.

We were to turn about immediately and make all possible speed to the southeast. Some 100 miles away, the Awatea, a troop ship carrying 5,000 American troops, was in danger of sinking. Her escort, an American destroyer, had encountered a surfaced U-boat and, in trying to ram it, had crossed the bow of the Awatea. The destroyer had blown up and sunk with all hands, while the Awatea had been left with her bow torn open. She was dangerously weighed down by torrents of water and her forward bulkheads were close to collapsing under the onslaught of the waves. If they did collapse, she would flood from stem to stern, plunging to the bottom with all on board.

Orders immediately went to the Kamsack's engine room to make more speed than we had ever made in the lifetime of the corvette. Soon, the whole ship was one mass of vibration. We ploughed through the Atlantic, smashing through the waves, throwing mountains of water aside as we hurled ourselves ahead. I marvelled at her performance—something like eighteen knots—and this from a ship which had never previously exceeded sixteen knots. We pounded on, all eyes focussed ahead, trying to spot the stricken ship. The seas were empty; not a ship in sight.

Shortly after 1600 hours, the lookout high in the crow's nest reported the first sighting. We were the first ship to reach her.

"Stand by," came her signal.

"We are preparing to abandon ship at any moment."

We felt helpless. Here we were, a 1,200-ton corvette, an oversized ship's whaler, alongside the towering Awatea. Yet we were her only hope if her crew was forced to abandon ship. We could see hundreds of soldiers in life jackets, lining her decks, probably thinking that we were a mighty slim chance for rescue. Messages flashed back and forth between the two ships. We closed in, making what preparations we could for rescue.

The Awatea's captain signalled that her bulkheads could give at any moment, and that the crew's only hope was to edge ahead toward the closest land, hope that the bulkheads would hold, and pray that other ships would get there in time.

The seas were calm, and the Awatea was able to move slowly through the water with virtually no added pressure on her vulnerable bulkheads. Time crept by. The two ships edged toward land.

Suddenly, a dot in the distance—another ship! Soon, the ocean was alive with ships, and we aboard the Kamsack no longer felt at such a terrible disadvantage in the dangerous situation. Awatea and her armada of escorts slowly made their way toward land and safety, and the wounded vessel made it to Halifax in one piece, despite a torn bow and seriously weakened bulkheads.

But there was a sad footnote to this event. Later in the war, I happened to read a dispatch from North Africa, reporting that a number of troop transports had been attacked in the invasion. Among them was the Awatea, which had been sunk. My thoughts went back to the joy I had felt at her earlier triumph against the odds, and I couldn't help the lump which formed in my throat.

MORE THAN ONE WAY TO CATCH A FISH

Depth charges were the major weapon against submarines during the war, and were used not only by destroyers and corvettes, but also by escorts, patrol vessels and aircraft. The Kamsack must have rolled hundreds of these 150-pound kegs of explosives over the stern, or fired them in ten-charge patterns, their settings fixed to go off at predetermined depths. The Canadian navy alone probably exploded tens of thousands of these powerful charges in its never ending war against U-boats. The results were often uncertain. Some charges destroyed or damaged enemy craft, bringing them to the surface; others were near misses, close enough to drive off the attacker; but countless others were dropped on doubtful or false targets. Old wrecks, whales, or schools of fish could be enough to send us all racing to Action Stations.

Late in the war, when the Germans came up with a breathing device, the snorkel, which allowed U-boats to remain motionless beneath the surface for long periods of time, all ships working in the English Channel were ordered to drop depth charges in a blanket coverage which, no doubt, gave great concern to the German navy, but also stirred up many an old wreck which had slumbered peacefully for centuries at the bottom of the Channel. The nonstop depth-charging was nervewracking for the off-duty watch trying to catch some rest, took a considerable toll on light bulbs, and tore quantities of insulation from the steel plating of the ship.

Depth-charging, however, produced a secondary effect in the rich fishing grounds off Newfoundland. We often found the ocean surface covered with thousands of fish, floating dead. Those caught in the centre of the explosions were mangled and torn, but those further out were simply killed by shock. It was a bewildering sight, and a common one. Perhaps it was because our fine old skipper was a Newfoundlander that we on the Kamsack took advantage of this odd byproduct of depth-charging to replenish our larders one tranquil day on the Banks. It was a perfect day for fishing: bright blue skies, brilliant sunshine, a fairly even sea. The Kamsack had just completed an assignment and was proceeding alone toward St. John's and a new mission. As we slid along, rolling and dipping our bow in the seas, the captain, who knew the waters well, gave clearance for the dropping of a single depth charge with a shallow setting. At the same time, the sea boat was readied for release and a sea-boat's crew mustered, armed with plenty of gaffs. The Kamsack revved up to maximum speed; the order was given to release the charge; and shortly afterward came the familiar rumble and the geyser of water shooting overhead. This time, we weren't worried about U-boats. Our only thought was of fresh fish for supper.

The Kamsack immediately wheeled in a tight circle and returned to where the charge had been dropped. We could already see hundreds of fish starting to float, belly up, around the centre of the explosion; and we slowed to almost a stop, releasing our sea boat into the thick of the fish. The boat's crew members didn't waste time on the mangled fish. They edged out to the rim of the explosion, where unmarked fish were rising to the surface by the dozens. Soon, they had happily gaffed the largest fish, cod, and rowed back to the circling Kamsack, the boat full to overflowing. In no time, we had hooked the sea boat, hoisted it aboard, and dumped onto the deck a mountain of beautiful, freshly-caught cod. For many of us,

raised far from the oceans and their bounty, this was an exhilarating sight. Our veteran fishermen from both coasts must have been somewhat less impressed, but just as eager to dig in. The fish were quickly cleaned, and turned over to the cooks, who had a great time preparing them for the evening meal. There were no limits on portions, second and third helpings were the order of the day. What a feast! Fresh cod off the Banks; as fresh as any fish ever caught, and plenty left over to squeeze into our refrigerator for another day.

A CHRISTMAS TO REMEMBER

The war made few allowances for festive days and holidays. More often than not, ships and their crews found themslves ploughing along in rough seas, days or weeks from home port. Conditions ruled out any attempt to be caught up in the spirit of a holiday, even Christmas. Survival was the overriding theme of the season, and a pervasive longing for home, family, friends and neighbours surged through us all. Other times, it was possible to bury our homesickness in the turmoil of war, but come Christmas, we could no longer sublimate our nostalgia for the Christmases of our childhood and youth. Still, ships' crews did their best to make the season a festive one. Aboard the Kamsack for Christmas away from home, we

opened parcels stuffed with woollen mitts, socks, toques, scarves, Christmas cakes and other foods—including, unfortunately, the inevitable cooked chicken, wrapped well but weeks old and smelling to high heaven! The celebrations continued as we joined all the other ships in port in tying to our masthead the traditional Christmas tree. After this ceremony, the youngest sailor on board, our boy seaman, "Smith," took over the role of captain for the day. Rigged out in the skipper's hat and jacket, he gave the welcome orders relaxing the rules of the ship for the day. Great pots of Christmas cheer, in the form of potent rum punch, soon appeared in the mess decks, and the ship came alive with singing and laughter.

The naval supply depot had sent a mountain of chickens aboard, and the cooks, no holiday for them, slaved all day to roast them in the small galley ovens, and to prepare the trimmings to go with them. In the late afternoon, each mess deck went off to the galley in turn to draw their quota: For our seaman's mess, that meant twelve large chickens. Only one problem: who was going to carve the birds? No one seemed to have ever carved a chicken, and I was the only one who had even a vague idea of how to proceed, having watched closely while my father carved our Christmas turkey. I was handed a carving knife of sorts and, to the shouts and encouragement of my messmates, I proceeded to carve all twelve birds. It went surprisingly well, and my buddies watched with delight as I piled their plates high with legs, wings, breasts, necks and stuffing. It was a fine Christmas dinner, washed down with pusser rum and spiced up with good company and good conversation; a meal whose warmth lingered long after we had cleared our plates away and prepared for sea: our sailing orders were for 2000 hours.

It was a Christmas memory that would sustain us even when December 25 became just another day at sea with a convoy.

NIGHTMARE ON DRY-LAND

News that a ship was so worn down that it required a major overhaul in drydock was cause for celebration among crew members, who were given long leaves and headed home. The day arrived when the crew of the Kamsack received the welcome order:

"Proceed immediately to Halifax for refit."

It was like a dream come true.

Soon, we were tied up under a big crane; the dockyard gangs swarmed aboard, and our ship was immobile in a matter of hours. Everything had to be examined and overhauled: guns, radar, ASDIC, wireless, and, above all, the engines, which had carried us faithfully through many a rough sea, with nary a falter, nary a breakdown.

As the refit began, so did the mad scramble to pack gear and head off to the frenzy of the wartime Halifax train station—destination: Montreal and points west. The Maritimers would have the easiest journey home, but many of the Kamsack's crew were bound for Montreal and even further west: Ottawa, Toronto, Winnipeg, Saskatoon, Edmonton, Vancouver, and dozens of smaller towns along the way. Some, heading home to northern Vancouver Island, would be six or seven days in transit, sitting up all night in a day coach and facing the same deadly haul on the way back. But it was long leave and we were heading home, and a long train ride didn't sound like much after what we'd been through.

The train, as always, was jammed with sailors, airmen and soldiers, heading home on leave, drafted to new bases, or picking up new ships. I noticed a group of young Royal Air Force cadets on their way to a flying base in Alberta; we struck up a conversation, and they told me they had never been out of England before. Even before they reached Montreal, they were overwhelmed by the vastness of Canada; I wondered what they would think after five more days on the train across the rest of Canada. I wondered what they'd think of Canada then! Life on the Maritime Limited was never dull, with drinking, gambling, and grabbing food and drink in whatever town we happened to reach for a minutes-long stop.

People slept in the aisles. Someone always had a guitar or a harmonica to provide the accompaniment to rousing sing-songs. And the train rolled along, mile after mile.

We were clacking away at top speed through a remote part of southeastern Quebec, with only the occasional village in a lonesome expanse of forests and rivers. It was late afternoon, and the hundreds of passengers had settled down to snoozing, reading or talking. I sat idly gazing out the window as the forest rushed by, a few feet away. Then, as if someone behind the curtain was pulling the strings, the whole world turned upside down. I could see several people running frantically across a clearing, all looking utterly terrified, as the engineer slammed on the brakes in an effort to slow our seventy-mile-an-hour speed. I know that I braced myself instinctively, and then it happened. We smashed head-on into a fully-loaded freight train.

Everyone scrambled out of the smashed car to find that we were, luckily, about twelve cars back of the engine. Up front, everything was a tangled mess. The two trains had collided in the middle of a bridge; the two engines had fused together in a mass of torn and twisted steel. Many of the freight cars from the front half of the train had been smashed and were lying in the river. The crews of both trains were dead; our baggage cars had been smashed and were on fire; and all the front passenger coaches were wrecked, their occupants injured and cut. Hundreds of people wandered, dazed, from the train to the little village with its few houses and one small store. The villagers tried their best to help the injured people until assistance arrived from elsewhere. Hours went by before a relief train made its way to us, and more hours elapsed as the injured were treated.

Finally, we continued towards Montreal; but the scene aboard the train was a far different one; no jawing, no singing; just solemnity and silence. There were none of the usual boisterous goodbyes in Montreal, as we headed to our westbound trains; just a numb realization that horror and tragedy can strike anywhere.

Forever after, I would re-live the tragedy every time I rode a train and the engineer applied even a gentle touch to the brakes. Sometimes, in the middle of the night, in a deep sleep, I would wake with a jolt, waiting for the horrible sound of steel on steel; cries of pain and terror; the torrent of broken glass; the thud of bodies, train seats and luggage collapsing in a chaotic heap. I still remember it.

GOODBYE TO THE KAMSACK

Knowing we were to leave Halifax the next morning at 0500 hours I made full use of my last precious hours in port, soaking in a hot, fresh-water shower and climbing into my hammock early for a full night's sleep—the last until we returned to port. Kamsack came awake in the pre-dawn darkness and we half-asleep sailors went about the business of readying the ship for departure, getting our lines in order, battening down everything on the upper deck, and checking the sea boats and life rafts.

Just as we were about to loosen our lines and cast off, a signal arrived on board, drafting me ashore for advanced training in anti-submarine warfare. Shocked and confused, I tossed my few belongings into my kit bag, grabbed my hammock, and numbly tried to say goodbye to my buddies; my shipmates, with whom I had shared so much over the previous eighteen months of turmoil, tragedy and triumph. What could any of us say in just a few moments about what we had experienced together during those long months of exhilaration and despair? A gruff farewell, accompanied by a hearty handshake.

At 0500, I made my way over the Kamsack's gangway for the last time, slung my kit bag and hammock onto Jetty Five, and stood there clutching my orders to report ashore.

There was little said as the last line was slipped, and the Kamsack slowly turned her bow away from the jetty and out into the stream. She slowly picked up speed, and I watched her head down Halifax harbour for the open sea and a new operation. For the first time since she was commissioned, back at the Oka Dock in Montreal, I was no longer part of her and her crew. As she passed McNab's Island and disappeared, I kept standing there on Jetty Five, quiet in the pre-dawn. I was overcome with loneliness —cut off from my ship and my shipmates. I felt a part of me would remain aboard the Kamsack forever.

I gathered up my belongings and trudged up the hill to the Stadacona Barracks and a new life ashore. It was a strange feeling, after all the months of barely surviving, to know that I was a dry-land sailor again, no longer faced with the stormy seas. Deep down inside me, I knew despite all the hardships there was only one place to be during the war—with a ship and shipmates.

But it would never again be the Kamsack and her crew.

I did see her again, even boarded her once, when she was tied up in St. John's. It wasn't the same. I felt like a stranger. Once parted from a ship, the old saying goes, a sailor is never part of her again. That's true; and it's one of the sad parts of life at sea.

Part 2 H.M.C.S. Caraquet

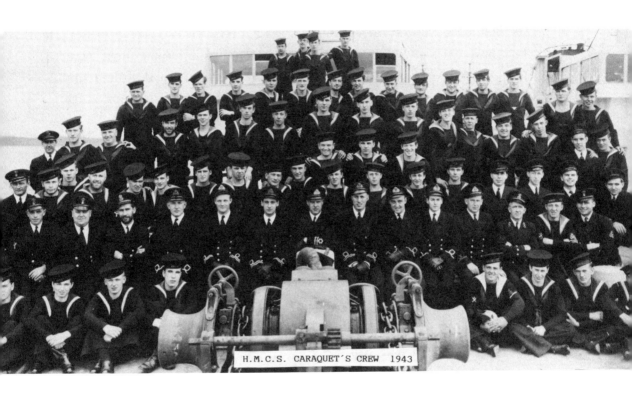

H.M.C.S. CARAQUET'S CREW 1943

New Ship, New Challenges

I wasn't a dry-land sailor for long. To my relief, I was soon posted to a new ship, H.M.C.S. Caraquet. Once again, I stood on Jetty Five in Halifax, kit bag and hammock beside me.

Naval life, particularly in wartime, has many customs and traditions. One of the most trying of these is the ostracism which always faces a new member of a crew. In my case, there was not only the problem of being a lone newcomer, but one who also presumed to break into the most sacred of navy enclaves—that of a tightly-knit, veteran crew, proud of their ship, and proud of their unity against all outside forces—including a stranger standing on their deck.

To make it even tougher on me, the Caraquet was also from the West Coast navy, had previously served in the Pacific out of Esquimault, B.C., and had a reputation for spit and polish. Captained by a reputedly tough and demanding skipper, she had just completed the famous run down the Pacific coast, through the Panama Canal, and up the South Atlantic into Halifax, to take up operations in the North Atlantic. I was joining her just before her first Atlantic assignment.

I watched the Caraquet come alongside, tie up very pusser and proper, then complete the ceremony by swinging the gangway into place, allowing me the questionable privilege of boarding her under the cold scrutiny of the crew, whose glances read:

"East Coast interloper!"

I can't imagine that the most exclusive club in the world would present a more formidable obstacle to overcome than these sailors presented to me. 124 firmly-established, closely-knit, true-blue West Coasters. I couldn't even dream that I would someday become part of this ship and her crew. All I could do was try to prove myself to this tough audience.

It didn't help matters that my shipmates quickly established that I wasn't a green recruit, but had had eighteen months of corvette life in the North Atlantic. Instead of tall tales about navy life, I faced a scaled-down version of coventry: a wall of cold indifference.

The icy treatment didn't last long. The testing period seemed endless at the time, but the thaw set in, and once it did, I found myself drawn into the life aboard the Caraquet. For the first time since I had left the Kamsack, I felt part of something again. One of the first crew members who broke the silence was a medic from Vancouver who served in lieu of a ship's doctor. John McTaggart and I established a rapport that deepened into close friendship as we shared the trials and tribulations of the Caraquet over the three years that followed. And it was through John that I met my wife—his sister—after the war.

The three ships in our group—Caraquet, Cowichan and Vegreville—were posted to special operations in the English Channel. One bitter January morning, we set our course for Horta, Faial in the Portuguese Azores. This British base, established under an ancient treaty with Portugal, was a welcome stop for refuelling and provisions before heading across the Bay of Biscay and up the English Channel to Plymouth, our British home port.

This was a different operation from anything I had ever encountered: no convoys to meet, to round up, to shepherd carefully across the vastness of the mid-Atlantic. Now we three ships were alone in the Atlantic. In daylight, we could look back at the next ship in line—Caraquet, as senior ship, was in the lead—and watch her plunge and roll a mile or so astern of us. At night, there was the tricky business of keeping station on each other without riding up on the quarterdeck of the ship ahead. As always, the main concern was an enemy submarine.

Within a few days after leaving the pack ice behind, we started to feel a change in temperature. We entered the Gulf Stream. It was my first experience of a warm Atlantic, after months of facing the fierce winds of the North Atlantic. With higher temperatures came strong, head-on gales and ever-mounting waves and it was back to wet mess-decks, soaking clothes and miserable living conditions—warm, but miserable. The waves made their way into every corner of the ship, and the chief torpedo man (who doubled as electrician) had nightmares about electrical circuits failing all over the ship, including those of the ASDIC gear.

As the head-on gales continued, day after day, we found our progress to Horta considerably slowed, as the ship's speed was cut in order to help her ride the heavy seas. As the daily mileage dropped, oil consumption rose. The captain and the chief engineer whispered anxiously about fuel reserves, the distance yet to be covered, and our chances of making it to Horta. Each day at 1200 hours, the latest calculations were made: it seemed we might just creep into Horta—with virtually empty fuel tanks.

The word from the Vegreville was less optimistic. The crew reported that she definitely didn't have enough fuel to get to Horta, and would likely run dry within twenty-four hours.

Our skipper ordered the Cowichan to prepare to take the Vegreville in tow as soon as possible; and soon the two ships undertook the nightmarish task of establishing a tow in the mountainous seas: securing a towing cable; trying to keep it from snapping. Just to shoot a line aboard in the fierce gale was a one-in-a-thousand chance, and even when the line was in place, it could be easily cut in two, as one ship plunged and the other reared. Through the brief hours of daylight, and into the darkness, the struggle went on. Then, more bad news: the Cowichan, too, was struggling to make her fuel last, and could no longer continue the attempt to take the Vegreville in tow.

Our skipper decided that the Caraquet would take up the challenge. The heavy towing rope was laid out in coils on the quarterdeck, and the Caraquet crept up alongside the Vegreville. It was incredibly difficult for the two ships to be kept close enough together to get a line across, and stay far enough apart to avoid a collision; but after many attempts, the first line went aboard the Vegreville, and her crew was able to slowly drag the thick towing hauser through the water and onto the fo'c'sle. We were connected to each other, and the Caraquet was ready to take up the slack and press ahead. As the two ships moved closer together, then veered apart, the tow line tightened as taut as a drum. Slowly, ever so slowly, we moved ahead, always expecting the line to snap, and snap it did.

Somehow, we groped our way to the Vegreville and laboriously passed over another line. It was like trying to thread a needle in the dark, but eventually we had her back in tow. We started to move ahead again, only to have the line break as the sea sent our ships plunging in opposite directions. On and on, through two endless nights, we stuck with the Vegreville, stopping constantly to pass fresh tow lines to her, then inching forward again.

We closed in on the Azores. As we came up between Corvo and Flores, the heavy seas flattened, the gales dropped, and all the problems of towing the Vegreville were gone. We picked up speed. As night fell, we thought we must surely be approaching paradise, with the heavy perfume of fragrant flowers from the nearby islands hanging heavy over the calm waters; the towering peak of Picos from the nearby island; and, just ahead, the breakwater of Horta, Faial. We had made it! We were all safely in port, and could enjoy a few hours of real life before heading north across the Bay of Biscay and down the English Channel to Plymouth.

We were supposed to be in Horta simply to refuel and provision before heading to Plymouth, our base of operation in the English Channel. Nothing was going to stop us from making the most of the time we had—especially when it came to gorging ourselves on piles of tropical fruit: bananas, oranges, limes and pineapples, long missing from our navy diet. Soon, we were swimming over the stern in the warm waters of Horta's harbour, and soaking up the warm winter sun. And within hours of our arrival, the ship was surrounded by countless numbers of small boats, as the residents of Horta came to meet the Canadian visitors and barter for anything we had that was made of wool. In return they offered us handfuls of cigars, bottles of Muscatel and Vino Porto, pineapples, bananas, Portuguese money and lovely lace handicrafts. No one on the ship could speak a word of Portuguese, and no one in the boats spoke English. The trans-

actions were carried out with a great waving of arms, pleasant smiles, peals of laughter, incomprehensible chatter and friendly gestures. Everybody on board got into the act, digging in kit bags and lockers for wool garments. An old turtleneck sweater, mitts, socks, toques, even pusser longjohns: an old, dirty turtleneck brought three bottles of Muscatel; a pair of well-worn socks was worth a handful of fine cigars; and as for the long-johns, they fetched three bottles of Vino Porto—fine old port. Before we sailed, our ship was stripped clean of anything woollen, and the Caraquet was somewhat deeper in the water from her load of wines, fruit and handicrafts.

During our first hours in Horta, the word was that we would not be allowed ashore, due to some quirk in the Anglo-Portuguese treaty which had opened Horta to allied ships such as ours. With all the absorbing activities going on around the ship, this prospect didn't seem so bad; besides, we were more or less resigned to the old navy routine of being so close and yet so far from touching ashore in a new port. In the meantime, while the captain was on frequent business ashore, the crew of the ship's boat, which ferried him back and forth, took advantage of the wait for his return, and slipped off to nearby wine shops, acquiring numerous bottles of the very fine wines. These they lashed to their legs (well-camouflaged by their wide bell-bottom pants) and innocently carried aboard, past the scrutiny of

the coxswain. Our wine stocks began to reach impressive proportions—all strictly against the King's Rules and Regulations!

Then word came through that the crew would be given a brief shore leave, one watch at a time. I wasn't on the first watch, but that was all right: there was nothing to do aboard but soak up the sun and enjoy the tranquility of a ship swinging idly at anchor in a tropical paradise.

Just before noon, we were shaken out of our torpor by the return of the first watch—a bunch of drunken sailors who tumbled aboard laughing, crying, fighting, vomiting and collapsing unconscious on the deck. The ship was in an uproar and we, the duty watch, could only stand by in utter amazement. How could this chaos have taken over in such a short time? The Old Man was furious, and wasted no time showing his wrath. He ordered the clearing of the lower decks—a rare event in our naval lives. The entire crew mustered on the quarterdeck, and he proceeded to read the Articles of War. It was indeed a sobering experience, even for the drunken lot who had triggered this action. The captain left no doubt in anyone's mind that he meant business; that we could face dire punishment at any time. Then, somewhat to our surprise, he announced that the other watch could also go ashore. None of us had to be told that there would be no re-peat performance of the morning's show.

Shore leave was a glorious experience. We wandered the lovely streets of the quiet Portuguese town with its tiled sidewalks; its smiling, friendly people; its women, wearing the traditional head-dress called a capot; its countless small wine-shops, where we stopped and (carefully!) sampled the best. We wandered up steep streets leading off into the coutryside, with postcard-perfect fields, lush hedges, and orchards heavy with fruit. Everywhere we went, groups of school children would surround us, giggling and chattering. At 1600 hours, we reluctantly headed back to the harbour to catch our liberty boats, but not before we had each purchased two bottles of fine wine and lashed one to each leg, to add to our already enormous stockpile aboard ship. Not a single bottle broke loose or shattered.

The day was not over yet. A group of us moved our wine to my AS-DIC compartment, deep down in the ship, right on the keel. Not wanting to risk a repeat of the earlier dressing-down (or worse), we closed the heavy water-tight door behind us and had one memorable wine party, on into the wee hours. Vino porto and muscatel flowed like water, and the ten of us sang ourselves hoarse. The sentimental old sweet songs carried us back to our homes and everything dear to us. Our hardened old fisherman-sailor, "Newfie," his haunting tenor full of the old Newfoundland ballads, poured out his heart in song until tears rolled down his cheeks and ours. We linked arms as we sang, in the deepest bonds of comradeship and friendship; and, all in all, it was a night that brought us together as never before.

Next day, before we pulled up anchor and headed north across the Bay of Biscay, I rounded up the last of my woollens and traded for still more fruit, which I took below and hung in my cool ASDIC compartment. I can still see the look of astonishment on the captain's face when, a week later, his rounds took him to my compartment. Staring at the stems of bananas, dozens of pineapples, and stacks of limes and lemons, he could only mutter something like:

"It looks like a bloody fruit store!"

But he didn't confiscate my booty. Another last-minute trade involved the exchange of yet another old sweater for a two-day-old kid, quickly named Bos'n Bill. Bill became the cause of many long strings of foul oaths as the captain stumbled over him on the way to the bridge. And the goat's other misfortune was his catholic taste. After chomping his way through boots, socks, books and everything else in sight, he tried out the batteries in the low power room. The battery acid did him in, and all we could do was give our matey a proper burial at sea.

Too soon, we had to leave Horta and sail into the gathering dusk. The lights of the town and hillsides—a thousand twinkling farewells—the 9,000-foot peak of Picos towering over us, and the heavy scent of what seemed like a million lilacs hanging heavy over the still waters, created a dreamlike setting. Then there was only the steady pulse of the engines as our three ships formed in line to steam between Corvo and Flores, and then north, toward England and back to the war.

The Caraquet was not always partnered with Canadian ships alone, as on that first visit to Horta. Throughout the war, Canadian ships often operated in concert with many of the allied navies. Our North Atlantic convoys frequently included Royal Navy destroyers and corvettes, U.S. Navy destroyers and blimps, Dutch submarines, and Coastal Command aircraft. In one operation along the French coast off German-occupied Bordeaux, our Canadian flotilla joined with a large Free French naval task force, including battleships. One convoy brought us into company with a Norwegian destroyer, and the great French submarine, the "Surcouf" showed up in many different waters. But it was the Royal Navy—its ships, its men, its naval ports and ageless traditions—with which we shared the closest ties.

We had always looked at the Royal Navy with a lot of respect for its superb ships, traditions, skills and morale. No navy was better at escorting convoys and destroying U-boats. At the start of the war, we had a feeling of inferiority: how could our small ragged fleet of corvettes, destroyers and bangors compare to the battleships Ramilles, Hood or Renown? As the war continued, our navy grew in experience and know-how: we came to feel we were on an even footing with the Royal Navy escort groups with whom we worked. Although there may have been some rivalry, we got on very well with our first cousins, the sailors of the Royal Navy. When Canadian ships were based for long periods in English naval bases, it was often difficult to obtain qualified Canadians to replace sick or injured crewmen, and it became common practice for the Royal Navy to lend us temporary replacements. This became a very revealing experience, both for us and the British sailors. We lived in two completely different worlds: while sharing a language and a common heritage, we sharply differed in philosophy and attitude. The Royal Navy had mellowed considerably since the days of press gangs, and the severe discipline of Drake and Nelson, but it remained a tough, hard navy, guided and led by its corps of permanent officers, chiefs and petty officers. The Royal Navy still lived by the long traditions of unquestioned discipline, part of which involved the bare minimum of consideration for the needs or comforts of the ship's crew. While the Canadian navy espoused some of this philosophy, developed during the days when our officers trained in Royal Navy establishments and served for extended periods on British ships, our navy's expansion saw many British traditions go by the board. Soon, ships were almost entirely manned by volunteer officers and men alike, with only a handful of permanent sailors scattered in a crew of 125. As well, the free-and-easy spirit of Canadian life was bound to erase from its armed services vestiges of their colonial traditions.

At one time, the Caraquet lost her yeoman of signals and was lent a Royal Navy yeoman, a permanent sailor. When he landed on board, the fundamental differences between us were immediately apparent, especially in terms of attitude to officers and their orders. The British yeoman was steeped in the long tradition of subservience to officers, whose commands were never to be questioned, always to be obeyed. It was with amazement that he viewed a typical Canadian sailor's reaction to officers. Some sublieutenant fresh out of the University, would try to tell a lifelong fisherman or former merchant marine when to throw a heaving line ashore:

"Look," the man would retort, "if you can bloody well do better, then you throw the bloody heaving line yourself!"

Our visitor would all but gasp with shock.

As weeks went by, the yeoman came to realize that we Canadians—while not as free-and-easy as the Australians—were far removed from the ways of the Royal Navy. It wasn't just the reaction to orders, either. Another major difference between our two navies was pay rates. We in the Canadian navy thought of our wartime pay as subsistence—equal pay for everyone of the same rank, but nevertheless a pittance compared to what most of us had been earning in civilian life. But in comparison to the Royal Navy, our salaries were positively exorbitant: an inexperienced ordinary seaman in the Canadian navy earned almost as much as a permanent, experienced, highly-skilled British yeoman of signals; a Canadian junior officer earned almost as much as a more senior British officer.

The quality of our food, too, was a major difference between us. We Canadians complained endlessly about the meals aboard ship, especially when we were expected to subsist on hardtack, sardines and salt cod. But our visiting yeoman made our situation seem splendid. Not only were the British navy's portions smaller, but the allowances for their food rations were also skimpier. They included almost no fresh milk, bread, fruit and vegetables, while our ships at least started out on a convoy with some fresh foods.

Once his initial shock had worn off, our visitor, confronted with these differences, became quite attached to our way of life; so much so that he decided to try to join the Canadian navy and remain a part of the crew of the Caraquet when we left for Halifax. This became his dream, and he talked of it constantly; however, as with many dreams, it was not meant to come true. Just as we were about to set sail for Halifax, the message arrived on board:

"Yeoman of signals Jones will report immediately to H.M.S. Devonport for further assignment."

He had no choice but to obey, and we were all sorry to see him go.

If meeting British sailors one-on-one was an enlightening experience, other experiences were not. One of the most distasteful duties we faced while in port at overseas bases was providing shore patrol to police the activities of our crew and any other Canadian sailors ashore. British sailors were amazed that Canadian ship's crews were stuck with such a duty; their patrols came from their shore-based navy. As for us, we hated the job: getting a patrol ready two hours after tying up; pounding the pavement until 0200 or 0300 hours; breaking up brawls between juicers (British sailors from the crews of ships); bringing in some wild-eyed sailor determined to smash a pub to bits; or pointing a drunken seaman to his ship.

There were frequent clashes between the Royal Navy and our shore patrols over what was considered proper etiquette. On one occasion, we had just secured our lines ashore in Plymouth when we received a naval message ordering us to provide a shore patrol, in dress Number One blues, at 1800 hours. I was designated the petty officer, and just before we headed ashore, I asked the officer of the day if we should change our uniforms. Rain was pouring down, and showed every sign of continuing well into the night. The officer quickly agreed that we should put on rainwear.

Our patrol marched up to the assigned area at the designated time, all of us rigged out in rain gear, to see the poor matelots from the Royal Navy patrols all decked out in their dress blues, sodden in the downpour. The captain in charge of patrols descended on us with fire in his eyes: had we not received his signal? Were we not aware of the meaning of the phrase,

"Number One dress blues?"

Had we not considered that it meant what it stated? What did we mean by arriving in rain gear? I tried to tell him that it hadn't made sense to dress for dry weather when it was pouring rain, but he didn't go for that logic.

"You bloody Canadians!" he bellowed. "You may run your little navy of corvettes and destroyers and mine-sweepers. But you would never be capable of running anything more than that!"

We stood there, warm and dry; calmly absorbed the blast from the brass; and tried very hard not to look sidelong at the "properly dressed" British sailors, drenched and miserable beside us.

Another patrol brought us more trouble than a lecture. Close to midnight on what had been a fairly quiet night, we were summoned to a pub where a Canadian sailor had apparently gone on a rampage, smashing his way through the building and overwhelming a Royal Navy patrol who had tried to subdue him. We arrived to find the pub in a shambles: glasses smashed; windows kicked out; a lone Canadian sailor threatening to massacre everyone in sight, particularly members of every juicer shore patrol around. He was a powerfully-built young man, hardly out of his teens, despite his wild appearance. We later learned he was ordinarily a quiet, withdrawn person, even when drinking. Something had evidently snapped inside him that night.

We approached him with caution, loath to get near the broken bottles he was brandishing. We hit on the idea of convincing him that we were his buddies; and that we would help him get back to his ship. Just as we were getting him settled down, a Royal Marine officer appeared on the scene and insisted that we take our wild Canuck to his headquarters to face charges for beating up his patrol. The young man, mad with drink, let loose a stream of invective against all things British, the Royal Navy and the Royal Marines in particular. We were dismayed at this spectacle; still, he sensed there was a difference between us and the juicers, and allowed us to ease him down the dark streets to the Royal Marine barracks.

Then, all hell broke loose. As it hit home that he was face-to-face with a Royal Marine captain, and about to be taken into custody by the Marines, he broke loose from us and laid into every marine in sight, biting and scratching, punching and kicking, until the office was a mass of rolling bodies, twelve on one. The cuffs were wrestled onto him, but he continued to struggle, the cuffs biting into his wrists, and spew oaths at his captors. Then, to our bemusement, the Marine captain ordered us to take our wild man back to his own ship to face charges:

"I've had my fill of Canadians, and this one in particular."

The sailor let us escort him down the cobblestoned streets, through the gates into the silent dockyard, and back to his ship, where we turned him over to the officer of the day with a brief description of the night's events.

The oddest turn of events was that the captain of the young sailor's ship, loath to have his sailor face the Royal Marine charges, somehow managed to smuggle him aboard another Canadian ship sailing for Halifax that day. We never did hear what happened to the lad, but we knew he could have been in irons for the duration of the war if the Royal Navy and Royal Marines had gotten hold of him.

Heroics, Hijinks And A Hiatus

A naval ship in wartime often faces missions with unexpected twists that have nothing to do with battle but demand a peculiar sort of heroism in themselves. The Caraquet and the cable ship Lord Kelvin combined on one such assignment.

One New Year's Eve, we set off from St. John's, Newfoundland: the Lord Kelvin was to repair a major break in the trans-Atlantic cable some 500 kilometres deep in the North Atlantic; we were to provide screening protection for the unarmed ship. The Lord Kelvin was a massive ship, fast and powerful; equipped to lay and repair trans-Atlantic cables.

Our first challenge was to match her speed. Once out of St. John's, we set our course in front of her, in a zig-zag screen, our engines pounding to produce maximum speed and somehow prevent the Lord Kelvin from riding up on our stern.

The crew of the Lord Kelvin seemed to know exactly where to locate the break in the cable; our task was to be ready when we got the message:

"Break located; ready to commence repair operations."

Then the most critical part of the assignment, for both ships: the Lord Kelvin had to stop in the North Atlantic and remain motionless and helpless for days, leaving it up to us aboard the Caraquet to protect her from U-boats while her crew carried out repairs to the cable. It seemed absurd for one small escort ship to be expected to provide any measure of real protection. The pre-arranged screening pattern required that the Caraquet continually circle the Lord Kelvin at close to maximum speed, laying off about one kilometre. Our watches were at ready alert; our gun crews closed up; our ASDIC constantly probing for the enemy, while the Lord Kelvin sat motionless, going about the business of repairing the break in the cable. It was a strange, eerie atmosphere aboard the Caraquet, as we gazed into our self-imposed circle at the helpless cable ship, and out into the silent ocean, where a U-boat could be laying in wait.

Then came the real test: the long, difficult hours of the night. It became more of a challenge to hold the circular screen; more of a war of nerves on us aboard the Caraquet, since we knew that if an attack were coming it would be during the night when a U-boat could more easily position itself against Kelvin—or the Caraquet, hampered as she was by having to maintain a continuous circle.

Daylight came, and once again we could see the Lord Kelvin, sitting motionless, her crew still working to complete the vital repairs to the cable. We felt a little better as we went around our screening circle, the ASDIC pinging out every few seconds; the lookouts peering for any sign of the enemy. As the hours and days wore on, the circular course—the constant leaning to starboard—so different from the convoy-protection patterns to which we were accustomed, began to make us a little anxious. As always happens during a monotonous activity, we began to sense just how alone we really were—two ships in a vast, empty ocean.

It was with mounting tension that we began another night of watching and waiting—surely the Germans would strike now—a night that seemed to drag on forever. As the first faint traces of dawn revealed the Lord Kelvin, her crew still intensely involved in the repairs to the cable, our frustration increased. How could the work take so long? We knew nothing of the immense technical problems involved in such repairs. All we could see through our glasses were men scurrying around on the upper deck, rolling the huge winding drums, which hauled aboard both ends of the broken cable, and splicing the two ends. No doubt the captain of the Lord Kelvin kept our captain fully informed of the progress they were making, but, as usual, we were told very little.

The signal flashed to the Caraquet:

"Repair completed; ready to proceed to St. John's."

A great cheer rose as the Caraquet moved out of her circular screening pattern to a position just ahead of the Lord Kelvin, then set course for St.

John's. The only ill-effect on us was a bit of dizziness after the days of circling; it took a bit of re-orientation for us to get used to the zig-zag screening the Caraquet normally provided.

Full speed ahead; and then, the narrow opening of St. John's and the rugged Newfoundland coast. The two ships slipped quietly into port, the Lord Kelvin heading to her usual berth, and the Caraquet taking her place alongside, on the South Side.

It was, on the face of it, a routine assignment; one which would surely never make the history books or even the rounds of tale-telling in pubs after the war, yet it was an experience none of us would ever forget. It was an experience of a quiet sort of heroism; a heroism of patience.

Another unforgettable experience of a different kind involved operational training, which faced newly-commissioned ships as well as veteran ships coming out of refit. Both these types of vessels had either new or overhauled crews who presumably needed the training. Ship's crews looked at these two-week periods of "workups" with mixed feelings of uncertainty and dread, because the experience involved being torn to shreds by the merciless techniques of a certain officer, let's call him Captain Bligh—and his equally sadistic staff.

They would drive us night and day, demanding impossible results, setting weird traps and springing unexpected assignments at unheard-of hours. They would think nothing of setting off an alarm for night action at 0200, after a killing fifteen-hour day of operations; and when something didn't go quite right, the blasts which came across the waters from Captain Bligh made the most hardened sailor cower.

In charge of as many as five or six ships preparing for operational duties, he demanded and got the absolute best from everyone on every ship, from cook to captain. When it was all over, it was with mighty sighs of relief, and no small feeling of pride at having survived, that we left the workup area and returned to Halifax for orders.

It was as a form of relief from the pressure of Captain Bligh that we on the Caraquet, during one workup, set out to "capture" H.M.C.S. Hepatica.

She was a veteran corvette from the North Atlantic convoys, with a crew who took great pride in having completed many tough assignments, and a captain who was well known for his tough no-nonsense command of a tough no-nonsense crew. The Hepatica was one of six ships including the Caraquet which had been sent to the vast, quiet waters of St. Margaret's Bay, just around the corner from Halifax, for two weeks of workups; and it was in this serene setting that we planned the capture.

The plot was largely hatched in our seaman's mess deck after over a week of non-stop battering by Captain Bligh and his ruthless staff. Day and night, we had tried in vain to respond to the barrage of commands he had flashed across the water: depth-charge run on the British U-boat Seawolf or Dutch U-boat Yll2; gun shoot; abandon ship; haul away kedge anchors in sea boats; fire at sea; save ship torn open after collision. We were worn to a frazzle, and, out of desperation, conceived a scheme to capture the Hepatica, thereby taking her down a peg or two, and giving us satisfaction which we sorely needed.

It was a simple plan: the Hepatica lay anchored about a mile from us; and in the wee hours of the morning, with all ships completely blacked out, a sea boat from the Caraquet with about fifteen volunteers would creep up on the target.

The night we picked was perfect, with torrents of rain and zero visibility. We had only the faintest idea how to find the Hepatica in the shrieking gale and pelting rain, but we kept on, rolling and pitching through the choppy waters, all eyes straining to catch a glimpse of our prey. We felt like caged tigers, wanting to shriek and shout and sing, but wary of making our presence known to anyone aboard the Hepatica, which might be very close indeed; it was difficult to tell in the pitch darkness. Finally, we found her, and crept up alongside without being spotted. By some great good fortune, we located a rope ladder down one side of the ship; slowly and quietly, ten of us mounted to her deck, still unchallenged.

Knowing her layout—it was the same as ours—we crept silently to where we would find the night watchkeeper. Sure enough, there he was, drowsy and unsuspecting. We quickly subdued him, found the other two men on watch, and got them under wraps as well. We now had command of the ship. To complete the capture, down the rows of depth charges we went, removing a dozen primers, vital to their firing. Then up to the fo'c'sle to remove the breech block from the four-inch gun, a most shocking loss for any proud ship. To the bridge, to take the ship's log. Then, back to the sea boat and off into the darkness before the alarm could be sounded.

We were bursting with glee after this escapade, and our three "prisoners" looked bewildered by the boatful of buccaneers who held them captive. What a night!

Later in the morning, our captain, sharing our triumph, signalled the skipper of the Hepatica, requesting that he send over a boat's crew to reclaim the ship's vital equipment and captured crew members.

From what we heard later, the "enemy" captain was fit to be tied, and infuriated with his crew for allowing such a deed to be perpetrated against the Hepatica. The crew of the beaten ship, not one to accept defeat without a fight, responded by sending four boatloads of their toughest sailors, determined to board us and pay us back. Their broom-handles, clubs and baseball bats were no match for our powerful fire hoses—we were ready for them—and they were forced to back off, vowing to seek revenge.

But the Hepatica made no further efforts to retaliate during the remaining days of workups. And whenever our paths crossed again, in distant waters and faraway ports, we always looked at our fellow corvette with renewed delight. It had been a moment of glory!

For corvette sailors, ingenuity was an essential element of survival, not only in such specialized—and controlled—circumstances as operational training, but during the endless weeks and sometimes months of confinement aboard small ships. As much as the comradeship of our shipmates kept us going in the worst of times, we were also driven to the breaking point by living like sardines in a can; jammed together with no hope of privacy. Looking back, I'm amazed that we all didn't break loose and go on rampages—like the unfortunate matey in Plymouth—when a long assignment finally came to an end and we made it ashore.

For many, the wet canteen or the warm confines of a British pub did much to restore the soul. An English pub, in particular, was a home away from home; as soon as the first liberty boat formed up for shore leave, the crew had already set their sights on their favourite pubs.

During the two years when the Caraquet was based in Devonport, the base in Plymouth, the pubs which survived the extensive bombing of this ancient port became regular watering holes for the thirsty, bedraggled sailors. One chap from Regina was so loyal to his pub that, during the entire two years we were in Devonport, he never ventured beyond the first street past the dockyard gate. On our very first shore leave, in the midst of a black-out, he had discovered the Chapel Pub, an ancient church which had been converted into a pub. He cherished the warm atmosphere, good ale and deep comradeship with fellow-sailors and the residents of Devonport; and when the Caraquet left the British base for the last time, he never really got over the loss.

While Devonport was no more than the Chapel Pub to one sailor, and didn't exist beyond a few steps from the dockyard gate, others ventured farther afield, exploring the historic seaport of Drake, the Armada and the Pilgrim Fathers; a community incredibly rich in the history of England's might at sea. Still others, like me, sought another outlet for our pent-up frustrations: walking. Nothing could quite equal the simple release to be found in covering mile after mile, stopping only when darkness fell and ex-haustion prevented me from going one more step. Tired as I was after one of these long hikes, I always felt renewed and restored afterwards; ready to face whatever new trials the sea and the war had in store for me. In fact, I could even sense some purpose to my life; not simply a blind push to sur-vive, but a feeling that my humanity, too, could endure.

Even with only a few hours of restricted shore leave before sailing again, I would leave the ship and walk away from port, out into the open country, and along country lanes or coastal paths, perhaps covering twenty miles before returning to the ship.

My various assignments in North America and Britain gave me great opportunities to exercise my chosen pastime. While in Londonderry, I crossed the River Foyle into neighbouring County Donegal, and walked for many a mile along the River Mourne, sometimes stopping to strip to my undershorts and plunge into its icy waters.

When our centre of operations was Portsmouth and The Solent, we landed at The Needles or Cowes on the Isle of Wight; and during the months we were stationed there, I completely covered the island on foot. As we shifted to other English ports—Weymouth, Falmouth, Torquay or Fowey—we walkers made the southern coast of England our own.

Over the two years we were there, we covered a good part of the coast, from Land's End to Portsmouth, and much of the Bristol Channel coasts of Cornwall and Devon. Two of us would catch a train out of Plymouth, hop off somewhere, like Barnstaple, in North Devon, find a bed-and-breakfast, slip out of our forbidding blue uniforms, and set off in some old civvies to walk, twenty, twenty-five, thirty miles along the rugged cliff-paths which ranged 200 feet or more above the Bristol Channel. On we would hike, returning only as darkness closed in on us. Then, we would grab a quick meal and collapse into bed, tired but happy. If we had two or three days, we would spend them all exactly the same way: walking, right up to the moment we had to catch the train back to Plymouth and the Caraquet.

Back on board, we were often quizzed about our disappearing acts, and some of our shipmates just couldn't believe we had spent three days doing nothing but walking. From their skeptical, amused glances, I'm sure they imagined we had several attractive young English ladies hidden away in the countryside!

When the Caraquet ended up in Lunenburg, Nova Scotia, for a mid-winter refit, I experienced walking which was quite different from the quiet lanes or rugged cliffs of the coast of Cornwall and Devon. In Lunenburg, I bundled up well, set off along the beaches outside town, and made my way, for miles and miles, along the magnificent rocky outcrops known as Blue Rocks.

There, with winter gales shrieking and turning my face to fire, with the great winter seas crashing and roaring over the rocks which didn't belie their name, I felt a deep communion with nature. The Caraquet was helpless and cold in drydock, the war and all its misery was far away; and here I was, tramping through deep snow over the beaches, with wind and wave at my very fingertips. Mile after mile I trudged, full of peace and inner harmony. Then, it was back to the temporary barracks to thaw out and await the evening meal.

Another unexpected respite from routine was a turn of events that took the Caraquet to Baltimore, Maryland, for refit. Most Canadian ships went to Halifax, Sydney, or smaller East Coast shipyards for refit, but some were affected by the terms of a treaty between Britain and the United States, established early in the war. Under the terms of the lend-lease agreement, Britain received fifty older U.S. destroyers in exchange for use of several of its island bases by the Americans. There were several other provisions in the deal, one of which involved a number of warships built for Britain. Some of these ships ended up in the Canadian navy and, under the terms of the agreement, their refits were carried out in U.S. naval yards. The Caraquet was one such ship, and her major refit was assigned to the huge naval base at Curtis Bay, Maryland, outside Baltimore.

The Caraquet and her war-weary crew, refugees from the bitter North Atlantic, set sail for this wonderful haven in the southern climes. Like the Azores, it was to represent another brief interlude in paradise for us; far from the icy seas; far from the war.

The base, with 20,000 sailors and a multitude of ships under repair, overhaul and construction, was a city in itself, offering every conceivable service: movie theatres, fire stations, shops, dry-cleaning establishments, laundries, tailors, everything a sailor away from home could need.

Right from the start, we Canadians were treated as guests and given first-class treatment and every privilege in the book. Nothing was too good for us, and after the rough life on the Caraquet and the austerity of Canadian naval bases, we felt we were in paradise. While our ship was dismantled and put back together, we moved to living quarters ashore. In a separate barracks, we ate in the regular messes, and we had complete run of the base. We soaked up the luxury.

The first shock came when we entered the mess hall for our first American meal. There were lineups of American sailors, but an officer insisted that we go to the front. That's the way it was for every meal during our stay in Curtis Bay. Guests came first!

There followed an even bigger surprise—the food. It was beyond our dreams to see the array of delicacies at every meal, served on china. Breakfast included our choice of a half-dozen different cereals, juices, hotcakes, bacon, ham, eggs in several styles, coffee, tea, milk, and mountains of toast—with seconds and thirds, if we wanted.

It was a bounty at lunch, too—salads, cold cuts, choices of sandwiches, soups and desserts. Dinner included beef, chicken, hamburgers, mountains of vegetables and a variety of desserts, including pies and cakes.

As if that weren't enough, the mess hall was open all evening for snacks, coffee and tea; scattered throughout the base were refreshment booths serving cold beer and soft drinks. We Canadians must have looked like half-starved refugees plunked down in a land of plenty as we ate our way through. It was hard to believe we were on the same continent, and in the same war!

We were urged to take full advantage of all the amenities on the base: twenty-five-cent haircuts, free first-run movies, cheap laundry and dry cleaning, and full purchasing privileges in naval commissary stores. We bought all kinds of U.S. Navy clothing at dirt-cheap prices.

By the time the Caraquet left Baltimore, the crew was decked out in U.S. Navy gob hats, white T-shirts, and other gear. We were overwhelmed by the generosity of the American sailors, and by their respectful interest in us. Many of them had yet to see active service and were impressed at how we had managed to survive years of service in the North Atlantic on our small ships.

The VIP treatment persisted even when we left and entered the base.

The American sailors had to pass through a half-dozen checkpoints and produce valid passes at each; we were greeted with a friendly wave and told to proceed. Could this really be a navy?

At every opportunity, we hiked the fifteen miles into Baltimore and enjoyed the hospitality of this southern city. We got into any theatre in town by paying the twelve-cent amusement tax, enjoyed free food and entertainment at any U.S.O., roller-skated with all the southern belles in the air-conditioned roller rinks; scooted off to tour Washington and the U.S. Naval Academy at Annapolis, and swam in Chesapeake Bay.

Life for Canadians was at an all-time high, and we had only one small gripe, the midsummer heat and humidity, which would have been fine if we had been able to wear tropical whites but they were never issued for the North Atlantic. We were all decked out in heavy blue wool uniforms. Our kit was great in the cold, and tolerable in a Halifax summer, but deadly in a city where the summer temperature reached 105 degrees and dropped into the nineties at night. We managed to find air-conditioned buildings on the base and in Baltimore, and the heat did little to interfere with our enjoyment. When the refit was complete, it was a sad day for all of us: rarely had we enjoyed such generosity.

Our course back to Halifax, and new operations, was a strange one: a sensational ride through the narrow channels of the Patapsco River, where we were often so close to shore that we could almost reach out and shake hands with the people wildly cheering us. Then down Chesapeake Bay to Baltimore. We entered the Atlantic off the U.S. naval base of Norfolk, Virginia, swung onto a northeasterly course; and revved up to full speed. There wasn't a sign of another ship.

In the second day of our passage to Halifax, as we dug our bow deep into the heavy seas, we received messages which directed us off course, and deeper into the Atlantic: a mercy mission.

A large floating drydock, being towed to Britain from the States, had encountered a severe storm. One of the drydock's crew had been injured; an urgent message for help had gone out. We were the closest ship. Late in the afternoon, we came directly up on the drydock, a massive structure, rolling and pitching ponderously in the seas as it moved ever so slowly, three knots an hour, toward Britain. The tug was a tiny object just ahead, its towing line dipping and tautening with the seas. It looked no bigger than a good-sized sea boat, and incapable of hauling the huge drydock.

Messages flashed back and forth between the seagoing tug, the drydock and ourselves. The injured man was in need of medical attention. Our crew made plans to launch our sea boat, go alongside, pick up the injured man, bring him back to the Caraquet, and then make all possible speed to Halifax and medical care.This was easier said than done. What felt like rough seas on the Caraquet would feel like a gale in a sea boat.

First, we who made up the boat's crew got all set after it was slung out and lowered to the water. As we rose and fell with the rising and falling of the ship, we awaited the critical moment when the coxswain would hit the release gear, dropping us onto the crest of the next wave; a critical decision, since we could either hit the water right, or be swamped, even lost. We hit it right, and were away, our oars digging into the waves which towered over us on all sides. It seemed a futile effort to row into such waves. We disappeared between two giant billows, climbing to the crest of the next, and flailing away with our oars, trying to make progress. Miraculously, we slid, climbed, bobbed and rolled our way toward the drydock. It was quite a ride. As we closed in, we were faced with the next challenge: coming alongside, picking up the injured man, and staying in one piece on the way back to the Caraquet.

It was a nightmare. We tried to keep some control over the boat and make it alongside. We came close only to be forced back by the waves.

The seas subsided for a moment. The drydock crew, who had lashed their man to a makeshift stretcher, lowered him toward us; we secured him in the boat, then started back to the Caraquet.

The danger wasn't over. Now, we faced being dashed against the steel sides of our own ship. But we made it. The hook clicked into the sea boat's lifting gear; our shipmates hauled away with gusto, lifting us cleanly out of the seas; we broke free of the waves, and, at last, were safe aboard with our precious cargo.

The poor fellow was in dreadful shape, and John McTaggart did his best to ease the man's pain while we made haste for Halifax. Word was sent ahead that we had an injured man aboard, and as we made our way up Halifax harbour and alongside Jetty Five, we spotted an ambulance awaiting our arrival. Within minutes, after securing alongside, the injured sailor was in the ambulance and on his way to the naval hospital. Everyone on board the Caraquet hoped for the best for him.

We didn't remain long in Halifax, and it was some weeks later that we returned to our home port, to learn that our mercy mission had not been in vain. The injured man was well on his way to recovery. Another wartime assignment that would never make the history books; but another memorable experience, nevertheless, for that drydock sailor, and for the crew of the Caraquet.

Last Months

In the final two years of the war, the Caraquet was the leader of a flotilla of seven ships based in Devonport and responsible for a variety of operations leading up to the historic invasion of Normandy: "D-Day". None of us on the lower deck were privy to any information about such crucial plans, but the rumours were that all the operational training we had endured—the endless drill on enemy aircraft recognition, for example—was preparing us for our part in the forthcoming invasion of the German-held French coast.

All this was months away. For the time being, the 31st Flotilla, headed by H.M.C.S. Caraquet and her skipper, Commander A.H.G. Storres, later to be decorated for bravery, took on a variety of assignments in the Channel, including mine-sweeping, offensive patrols, and large-scale pre-invasion exercises.

All was not preparation for life-and-death warfare. During her years in the English Channel the Caraquet often dropped anchor in The Solent, the waters sheltered by the Isle of Wight and located within a stone's throw of Portsmouth and Southampton. These waters were a traditional refuge of ships from the storms of the unpredictable Channel.

Stopping in The Solent usually meant that we had to stay aboard, although at times the captain arranged for a liberty boat to come alongside and take us into Portsmouth for a few hours of shore leave. A few times, we took matters into our own hands, rowed our sea boats to the nearby Isle of Wight, had a ball game in the shadow of The Needles—the magnificent sand cliffs of vivid orange, red and yellow. During one of these outings, a few of us wandered away from a game in progress and set off up a country lane to a sleepy country pub, where the ale flowed like water.

In the months leading up to "D-Day", and following it, The Solent became one massive anchorage for every manner of ship: battleships, cruisers, monitors, destroyers, corvettes, mine-sweepers, mine-layers, and landing craft of every shape and size.

The Solent was laid out like an oversize parking lot in a shopping mall: every ship that entered the relatively narrow waters was assigned its particular "parking" spot. Anchors were dropped, and ships lay swinging in endless lines. At night, the blackouts created hazards; but ships continued to come and go despite the lack of visibility.

On one occasion, the Caraquet, on her way back to England after operations along the French coast, entered The Solent from the Spithead end. A signal was received from shore to proceed to the anchorage and drop anchor in our assigned spot for the night. After the initial groans—no shore leave again—we resigned ourselves to the inevitable. The captain carefully directed the Caraquet to her allotted spot and, equally carefully, gave the order to drop anchor. Down it rattled, and soon we were swinging peacefully in the calm waters of The Solent.

The Caraquet settled down to life at anchor. The only sound was the hum of our electrical systems and the only movement was the occasional ship coming into the anchorage or getting under way to head out into the

Channel. We prepared for a peaceful night.

No one noticed that our anchorage spot was tight up against the main channel, with no other ships intervening; this was to become significant.

At 0200, the ship silent and asleep, with only the night watchkeeper awake, disaster struck. A large and cumbersome U.S. Navy Landing Craft (LST) was making her way down the narrow main channel, lumbering along in the pitch dark. Only one problem; she wasn't on course. Somehow she had wandered out of the main channel and was headed for the nearest ship—the Caraquet.

If she had hit us square on, we would likely have split open and sunk to the bottom of The Solent. As it was, the LST struck us a crushing blow, well up on our starboard side, at about a forty-five-degree angle. One moment we were a sleeping ship. The next a frightening blow: steel on steel, well above the water line, and right into our seaman's mess deck.

The blow just about drove the ship bottom-side up. I thought we were goners. The deck became a screaming, scrambling chaos. We stumbled around in the dark, not knowing what had happened or what might come next.

After its initial blow, the LST bounced down our starboard side in a series of secondary blows, and slid off into the night.

Pandemonium inside the Caraquet continued for some minutes, until we realized we were still afloat; that we were in no danger of sinking despite the gash in the ship's side; that we had been the victim of a hit-and-run LST.

Then, our skipper took over.

He bounded up to the bridge in his night attire, grabbed a loud-hailer, turned it up to full volume and after establishing that the captain of the landing craft was listening, proceeded to put on the most amazing display of rage and splutter imaginable. Using oaths we had never even heard before, he dressed down the U.S. Navy captain in the most devastating terms; and laid it on in one long, uninterrupted diatribe, never giving the other captain a chance to tell his side of the story.

Recovered from our panic, we stood in groups on the deck, thoroughly enjoying every moment of the tirade, and already starting to speculate on the amount of time it would take the dockyard to repair the gash in the Caraquet, and how many days' leave might be in store as a result.

We weren't in the dockyard long. The steel-plate workers would soon have a patch riveted into place over the gash, and we would be ready for sea. The mishap was worth a couple of days' leave, anyway—plenty of time to spin the yarn of Commander Storres and the United States Navy Landing Craft over a tankard of ale.

A serious part of the last months of the war at sea was the presence of mines. Vast minefields were strung around the British Isles, in the English Channel and elsewhere, as defences against submarines and prowling ships of war. The Germans, using large mine-laying submarines, also placed minefields in the main convoy routes, off important ports such as Halifax and St. John's, and thick along the French occupied coast.

Some were traditional mines: huge steel balls, loaded with explosives, covered with ugly horns, and set off by trigger mechanisms. Yet others, developed during the war, were magnetic mines, set off by the passing of a steel-hulled ship; still others were acoustic mines, designed to be detonated by the sound of engines. Countless ships fell victim to these deadly weapons, and, for many years after the war, mines continued to float free in the oceans, destroying ships, and exploding on beaches when washed ashore.

The Rules of War required that mines be anchored—as many were— but it was not uncommon to come across a horned monster bobbing loose, ready to explode.

Ships such as the Caraquet frequently engaged in the touchy business of clearing mine fields by cutting the mines from their anchored positions in the depths, and deliberately exploding them, sometimes uncomfortably close to the ship. Once in a while, our cutting mechanism reappeared on the quarterdeck with a huge mine tangled in its cutters. The crew would race forward, terrified that the stern was about to be blown to bits, but the captain knew how to handle the situation. He stopped the ship, ordered the gear be made loose and commanded us to group together far forward. The ship went from full stop to full speed ahead. We all held our breath as the gear and its entangled mine were dragged astern. The trick was to avoid an explosion until we had opened up a margin of safety. Somehow, we always did.

Several times, the mine went off a stone's throw from the stern; in the shattering roar that followed, mountains of water poured down on the ship, leaving us feeling that we were being torn apart. Lights were broken all over, steel rivets were forced loose. It was unnerving, and we developed a phobia about taking up our cutting gear, lest yet another mine be dragged onto the quarterdeck.

Floating mines were another matter. A lookout would report:

"Floating mine just off the port bow!" and then the fun began.

The captain gave permission for the entire crew to take up arms and fire on the monster while he manoeuvered the Caraquet to keep her out of harm's way. While our ship circled the mine, the regular guns' crews started in with the Bofors anti-aircraft guns, while others took up positions with a number of rapid-fire Sten guns. The main naval gun on the fo'c'sle also swung into action, and all other crew members, armed with rifles, were strung out along the top deck. Some of the officers even brought out their pistols to add to the barrage. With this outpouring of firepower, one would have thought that it would be a quick end for the mine, but that wasn't always the case. The mine was low in the water. Only a portion of the upper part was visible. The surge of the sea would keep the mine bobbing in a most maddening manner; most of the time, it was out of sight.

The scene was out of an old-fashioned shooting gallery: the little ducks going up and down, in and out of range. When we succeeded in hitting the

mine, the bullet would usually ricochet off the steel casing. Not that the difficulty of the challenge deterred us in any way: the din and excitement of a shoot-out (the term we used to describe these attacks) was something to behold. For the crew, danger was soon ignored as our schoolboy glee took over and we unleashed all our emotions, filling the seas with our shots, shells and shouts. As the shooting reached a frenzied peak, the captain looked on in high amusement at his crew's efforts.

The climax was sometimes disappointing. One moment, the mine was there; then, it simply slid beneath the waves, gashed and silent. Much more satisfying was when someone's shot hit a vital spot and the mine exploded with a sky-high geyser of water. The mighty roar would be echoed by our own cheers of jubilation. We would sweep up all our spent shells, dump them into the sea, return our armoury of guns to their places until the next shoot-out, and set off again on our assigned course.

Despite these lighthearted "target practices," we all knew that a cataclysm was upon us.

Assignments became more intense, and the details of the invasion of France eventually reached lower-deck sailors. We knew what it was like to be bombed; to see German aircraft shot out of the sky; to be poisoned by the chemical fog laid over Portland harbour with the objective of protecting us; to watch huge mines erupt in the crowded harbour jammed with invasion craft and naval vessels like ourselves. Nothing we had experienced thus far could prepare us, the crews of the Caraquet and her fellow bangors in the 31st Flotilla, for what was to come.

As it turned out, we led the procession of battleships, cruisers, destroyers and landing craft destined for the French coast. We felt proud to be in the vanguard, leading all the way to the beaches of Normandy, where the bombing went on throughout the night; where aircraft fell in flames, and great fires blazed in the pre-dawn darkness. Here, off Omaha Beach, we experienced first-hand the now-famous first hours of "D-Day", when it seemed that the American troops on the beaches could not hold.

Then followed days, weeks and months of almost unceasing operations: exploding mines: driving off German aircraft, which flew low over the vulnerable invasion fleet at night; patrolling; escorting—the assignments that came the way of a naval ship in the thick of war.

We reached peaks of excitement, depths of fatigue and despair as the Channel war went on; and, yes, once in a while, we sensed that we were all part of something much bigger than ourselves; part of history.

For many weeks, the fighting on land was still almost visible a short distance inland, as the battleships stood off behind us, their mighty shells roaring over our heads toward the German front lines. Allied aircraft continued to attack. Then, as the fighting gradually moved inland and the constant rumble grew fainter and fainter, we made our way into the newly-freed ports along the French coast, often within days of the end of fighting. Some ports, such as Le Havre, La Rochelle, St. Malo and Cherbourg, held out for some time. In mid-July, Cherbourg fell, and after being held off this great Atlantic port for days, the Caraquet pointed her bow at the narrow opening of the 100-foot sea wall and moved into the anchorage.

The main port area had been cleared of Germans two days before, and fighting was fierce in the hills surrounding the port. Accustomed to the uncertainty of sea warfare, we aboard the Caraquet were overwhelmed by the reality of land warfare going on all around us. A tragedy brought it closer.

One evening, as our flotilla took up night operations in the anchorage area, ready for anything, two sailors from another ship, desperate to touch dry land, bundled up their clothes, slipped over the side of their ship, and swam the short distance to shore. They had barely started up the beach when they both stepped on German land mines and were instantly killed. A few steps of freedom, and their lives were over.

As the weeks after "D-Day" continued, we knew the war was slowly moving to its climax. But until that happy day, we were kept busy along the French coast.

Late one night, we were heading back to Cherbourg to await further orders; steaming alone, with all sea watches closed up. The seas were calm; all was silent, except for the pulse of our engines and the sound of the Channel waters as we cut through them. It was a dark night, with scattered clouds, and as we sailed on we thought this would probably be quite an ordinary night.

When the watch changed at midnight, a young sub-lieutenant, who had gone directly into the navy from the University of Toronto, took over the watch. The ship and all her crew were now his sole responsibility, and he loved the role though he was a less-than-inspiring figure as he pranced pompously about the bridge. One other characteristic of our young leader: he was rather short and plump, and the first time we laid eyes on him, we gave him the nickname "Lardarse," which, needless to say, he didn't appreciate. Well, Lardarse would have his moment of truth shortly after midnight, off the French coast.

The heavy clouds gradually dissipated and a full moon started to rise, low on the horizon. As Lardarse prowled the bridge, basking in his temporary command of the Caraquet, he gazed aft straight into the brilliant face of the moon. That did it. At once, he sprang into action, pushing all the alarm bells and screaming for the gun crews to train all their guns aft on the enemy. The quiet Caraquet was thrown into turmoil. Alarm gongs clanged, off-watch crew scrambled, still half-asleep, to their action stations; and everyone had that awful feeling of danger close at hand. From my ASDIC station on the bridge, I had a first-hand exposure to the rapidly developing situation as the skipper arrived from his cabin below the bridge and demanded to know what was happening.

In the moments between the initial spotting of the "enemy" and the gathering of the crew to full Action Stations, the clouds continued to disperse, and the rising moon, still hanging low over the horizon, broke into full radiance. It was a beautiful sight, a great full moon over calm waters just off the French coast. With it came the dawning realization that the rising moon was the enemy. (Lardarse's enemy, at any rate!)

If there was a sense of relief among the crew, there was also a rumble of annoyance as we realized that Lardarse had dragged us out of our off-watch sleep to have a look at the rising moon. The captain, for reasons of his own, chose the route of diplomacy.

"Well," he remarked mildly, "better not to take any chances."

Unusual enemies aside, we never knew, from day to day, where we might be going next, or where we might end up. Day and night, week after week, we plunged into new waters and new operations.

As the war intensified, it seemed that we would never find a moment to call our own; a moment when the war wasn't everything. Yet there were such moments, rare as they were.

On one operation, we were sent to the outer reaches of Brest, at the mouth of the Loire River. We had penetrated to the heart of the vast German U-boat pens, from which the submarines headed out into the Atlantic. As we explored the naval base in our sea boats, we marvelled at the submarine pens, with their concrete roofs, 100 feet thick, untouched by the hundreds of bombings which had devastated the old city of Brest.

We were ordered to remain at anchor for the night close to shore, in the outer harbour ready to set off at dawn. A more peaceful setting than the sheltered outer reaches of the Loire would be hard to imagine: the waters were calm, the sun was setting behind the low hills, and the silence was all-pervasive. It was a moment as close to utter tranquility as we had come to in many a day. As the Caraquet swung at anchor, we settled down to an evening of catching up on some rest.

Then, in the long summer twilight, we noticed small fishing boats approaching from the nearby shore, and soon we were surrounded by many of the local Brittany fishermen. They were full of friendly chatter, and eager to share their boatloads of shellfish—mussels, scallops, periwinkles—and crabs. They agreed to barter for our Canadian cigarettes, bars of chocolate and soap. Soon, they were hoisting on board whole sackfuls of periwinkles, mussels, and armfuls of crabs. The deck of the Caraquet took on the atmosphere of a fish wharf. Excitement swept the ship as we rounded up every pot and old bucket. Then to find room on the tops of the galley stoves to cook them! In no time, we had cooked shellfish fit for a king.

All over the Caraquet, sailors were busy prying every delectable morsel from the shells. It was a feast to be remembered. As fast as we finished off one batch, more sacks of seafood were hoisted on board, cooked, and devoured. One huge pot was kept for crabs, which were gradually added to the evening's banquet.

As the hours passed, the French fishermen began to bring us boatloads of wine to wash down the shellfish, and then, dessert: huge baskets of freshly-picked strawberries, which we ate in great handfuls, washed down with wine.

Here on this war-battered coast, in sight of the massive U-boat pens and the total destruction of Brest, we had a feast of fantastic proportions—cooked in a rough-and-ready manner, but unsurpassable. Periwinkles, scallops, crabs, mussels, French wine and strawberries: our crew would never forget this evening.

As if to add a touch of irony, the fishermen, thinking to please us, started to bring us boatfuls of German rifles picked up after the recent battle for Brest. They thought we wanted to add to our collections of war memorabilia. Periwinkles and wine were more to our taste that twilight.

Throughout the war, we had all heard stories and rumours about the secret weapons the Germans were intending to use against England to terrorize the people into submission.

In the summer months of 1944, the stories turned to reality, as flying bombs were launched across the narrowest part of the English Channel, to descend on London by the hundreds. Although other areas, along the route from the Pas de Calais to London, suffered from the attacks, London was the target, and its residents faced yet another long siege.

In mid-July, after her assignments along the French coast, the Caraquet was escorting a large convoy of merchantmen from the coast back to England. In the strip of the Channel that was soon to be known as buzz-bomb alley, we had our first encounter with flying bombs.

With German installations in the Pas de Calais ready to launch and direct the bombs into the heart of London, this part of the Channel became the crossing point. The bombs were launched from their pads, their timing mechanisms set to shut off over London, then driven to their targets by fearsomely noisy engines. Their grimmest features were the great flaming tails which flared out of their rear engines, and flamed out in billowing, fantastic shapes as the contraptions powered their way to their target.

As soon as we entered buzz-bomb alley with our convoy, a group of flying bombs howled out of the darkness, above the convoy. Their awesome roars, combined with their eerie, flickering, flaming tails, made them a terrifying spectacle as they flew their predetermined course to London.

Shortly afterwards, ten or more of them came out of the darkness in a group. This time, all the ships opened up on them with their anti-aircraft guns, and it was a heartening sight to see at least one of them come plunging down, disabled, to explode in the sea with a great roar and a sheet of flame. It was our first success in preventing a few of the bombs from reaching London; later, others were destroyed along the land route.

During the weeks that followed, we saw many of these frightening bombs heading in streams across the Channel to terrorize London.

I was to have the questionable privilege of seeing them even closer. Some weeks later, with the Caraquet tied up in Portsmouth for forty-eight hours, I caught a train to London. No sooner had I walked out of Paddington Station than I found myself face-to-face with the awful destructiveness of the flying bombs. The air-raid sirens screamed their warning as nine of them came roaring in on central London from the southeast, each bomb with its terrifying roar and trailing sheet of flame. Their speed was not exceptional, and, as they loomed closer, anti-aircraft guns on the outer fringes of London tried to bring down the monsters before they reached their target, the heart of the city.

The Germans had hoped the flying bombs would paralyze London, but their efforts were fruitless. Despite the onslaught, life went on; people strolled the streets; buses moved along; stores and hotels operated as usual; and London seemed determined not to give in to this latest terror.

And I mean never.

First, there were the nine bombs, which eluded the anti-aircraft guns and passed a park to which I had walked from the train station. I ducked behind a huge oak tree, and, along with several other people who had sought shelter, watched with amazement and terror. The most terrifying moment of all was when the roaring engines shut off. Everyone knew this was the sure sign that, in about five seconds, the bombs would dive and explode. Three of the nine followed this pattern, shutting off their engines nearby and diving, with deafening roars, into the surrounding neighbour- hood. The whole section of the city was shaken, but shortly afterwards came the all-clear signals, and people reappeared on the streets.

I came out from behind the tree and caught a bus to visit friends in Lewisham, in the southeast part of London. As I arrived in the Ladywell district, another flock of bombs had just exploded: many blocks of the area had been destroyed, and more than 160 people had been killed by a single bomb exploding in a dense shopping area. My friends had left the neighbourhood, and I found myself alone in London with a steady procession of flying bombs arriving, hour after hour. I could hear them constantly, some far away, some closer, some very near.

As night came and darkness descended, bombs continued to arrive from the southeast. Now, in the darkness, their roaring engines and great flaming sheets of fire took on a diabolical cast. At midnight, I stood alone in Leicester Square as a bomb approached. There it was, low over the roof-tops, a monster sent by the very devil. Its roaring engine shook the build-ings surrounding the square; then it shut off and there were a few mo-ments of piercing silence that seemed a lifetime. Finally, it exploded, just across the square, behind the first row of buildings. It was as if the end of the world had arrived, and when I continued toward my hostel, I was in a state of shock.

The following day brought more of the same: bombs roaring in from the southeast, air-raid sirens screaming, engines shutting off, great explo-sions. In the afternoon, I went to a movie theatre crowded with Londoners —life did go on—and while I can't remember the name of the film, I'll never forget sitting there in the darkness and hearing a flying bomb approach, only to shut off directly overhead. A sickening few seconds of silence, and the bomb exploded two or three blocks away. The theatre shook; plaster and dust showered down on the crowd; but no one left, and the movie continued. It was as if nothing had happened.

During those two days, eight to ten of the flying bombs arrived every hour, shattering many sections of the city and killing hundreds of people. But London never gave in to this latest and last act of terror.

Homeward Bound

We had little doubt, in the lovely spring days of April and May of 1945, that the war was close to an end. The news pouring in from every front told of total defeat for the German armies; defeat for the German U-boats; defeat for the German air force. Even in the English Channel—our corner of the war—everything was winding down.

But for the Caraquet it was not quite over. There always seemed to be one more operation. As it was announced, on May 7, 1945, that V-E Day would be declared the following day, we received orders for one last mission. We were to be part of a British task force of cruisers and destroyers landing an army group in the German-held Channel Islands. These British islands on the coast of France had long been an annoyance to ships operating along the French coast, and Germany's heavy coastal assault guns were always ready to toss a few shells at any ship which wandered within range. We had always given them a wide berth, but now, as we set off on a voyage of liberation, we were going to see them at close range.

It was still uncertain if the Germans holding the Channel Islands had surrendered, despite the end of the war on the Continent. For this reason we set sail with a large group of cruisers, destroyers and armed soldiers. To get into the spirit of V-E Day the captain ordered a double ration of rum—splice the main brace—as we listened to Churchill on the ship's radio, talking about the end of the war.

As we closed in on the coast of Jersey, one of the main Channel Islands, there was still some fear that we would be on the receiving end of German heavy-artillery shells, and that British soldiers might have to fight a final battle to get ashore. But as daylight took over, no shells came our way, and the landing craft, crammed with soldiers, steamed right up to the beaches, unmolested. There, we found ourselves faced not by hostile German soldiers but by joyous citizens, liberated after years of German occupation. The German soldiers, in turn, submitted themselves as captives without a shot being fired. This was the story throughout all the other islands; and, very soon, we on board the Caraquet were caught up in the surging spirit of the end of the war.

However, we didn't linger in Jersey. The next stop was the nearby island of Guernsey and its lovely port, St. Peters. All our pent-up feelings united in a bursting surge of total happiness. No more war! It was a grand sharing of the deepest of all emotions: joy at the coming of peace.

It was a celebration to remember. The entire population of St. Peters climbed into small boats and headed out to our anchored ships to greet us as heroes. Soon, we were surrounded by joyous people, singing, cheering, waving flags and conveying to us their unbounded gratitude for their liberation from the Germans who had held their island. Some clutched the first edition of a two-page newspaper, the first since occupation, bearing the huge headlines: **"Guernsey Liberated!"** and **"The War is OVER!"**

The cheering continued into the soft spring evening, as if the people of Guernsey felt that this moment mustn't be allowed to end. We on the Caraquet were totally caught up in the emotions of the hour. Here we were, after all the years of war, despair and hardship; here we were, seeing the fruits of our efforts—the liberation of a captive people. It was one of the few times that we knew it had been worth it; that our efforts had been part of the victory. The celebrations went on far into the night, as some of the residents' boats went ashore and returned with small gifts for the sailors. But the greatest gift of all was the splendour of their feelings for us. We had all come together in victory, and in peace. There would never be another day to equal it.

The following day, we headed back to Plymouth and new orders: the Caraquet was kept busy for months, clearing up mine fields and exploding mines. But for me, it was all over (or so I thought) in early August, 1945, when my discharge papers arrived on the Caraquet, ordering me to report to H.M.C.S. Niobe in Greenock, Scotland, the Canadian navy's overseas base in Britain.

And so this grizzled old veteran of twenty-five arrived at Niobe, an ancient stone fortress which had once been an insane asylum—a fact in which we "inmates" took rather ironic pleasure. I wasted no time trying to find out when I would be released; put aboard a homeward-bound vessel, that is. At first, the response was vague; I began to suspect that I wasn't going anywhere. I requested to see the captain, and he broke the grim news to me. His hands were tied; he was responsible for getting thousands of sailors home as quickly as possible; he desperately needed some experienced hands like me. Protests got me nowhere. I was stuck in Niobe, helping to organize shiploads of homeward-bound veterans, whose one or two years of service apparently meant more than my five.

The only thing that kept me sane was the setting of Niobe, tucked in the beautiful hills overlooking the River Clyde and set off by the vast, deserted moors of Renfrewshire, stretching away to the horizon. At every opportunity, I set off on foot or on an old bicycle to cover twenty, thirty or even forty miles of these magnificent moors. Often, I walked or rode the entire day without seeing any sign of life except for grazing sheep, which looked up at me in surprise as I passed.

The other saving grace of Niobe was the library, crammed with just the books I had always wanted to read. I practically lived there during the long evenings, before heading off in the darkness to the Nissen hut I shared with four other sailors. The hut was unheated, and the only way to offset the cold was to plunge into one of the massive eight-foot tubs which stood, row on row, in the huge bathroom of the old asylum.

In many ways we felt isolated from the terrible events still transpiring in the Pacific, but in early August, 1945, word came back that a horrible bomb had destroyed Hiroshima, Japan, and that a second explosion had devastated the city of Nagasaki. The war really was over. It would be some time before I realized the terrible human cost of this peace

The captain of Niobe, an old hand and very much in touch with the mood and emotions of his veterans, started things moving. He sent several of us up the Clyde to the large Kelley estate to spend the day cutting and dragging old timber from the forest, loading it on trucks, and hauling it back to Niobe to build the biggest bonfire in Britain.

In the middle of the night, word reached Niobe that the war was officially over. In minutes the entire base was awake and hundreds of sailors were parading around in their underwear. The entire Niobe band, holding their instruments, were similarly clad, as was the captain, who was hoisted onto the shoulders of a few sailors to lead the parade.

The following day, we laboured in a downpour to make ready for the festivities. Huge kegs of local beer—each keg must have held fifty gallons were set up; there was enough to satisfy the thirst of half of Scotland. Alongside were tables to handle the tons of food, specially prepared for the occasion. As evening approached, the rain stopped and the citizens of Greenock, invited to share in our celebrations, started to arrive in hordes. The bungs were knocked out of the beer kegs; the beer began to flow; and a torch was put to our mighty bonfire.

It was a glorious evening of celebration; vast quantities of food and beer were consumed; great sing-songs were led by the Niobe band; and an all-night dance was held in Niobe's one large indoor hall. During all this singing, drinking, dancing and carousing, there wasn't a single fight or a single ugly incident. Everyone simply wanted to celebrate.

Three days later, when we had somewhat recovered, the captain arranged a climax to all the victory celebrations. He hired the largest of the old cruise ships which, in peacetime, carried the citizens of Greenock along the Clyde on Sunday cruises to their favourite beauty spots. He packed the boat with food, beer, the Niobe band and the entire naval population of Niobe; and we all set off down the Clyde and up the Kyles of Butte, one of the wildest, most beautiful sights in all the world. After our wild party, this was one of the most renewing experiences of our lives. We were overwhelmed by the beauty of the forests, the waters, the sky—the peace and quiet as we glided along. Beer was consumed, food disappeared, the band played soft melodies, and there was even some dancing in a small clearing. But, for the hundreds upon hundreds of us, crowded together, it was the loveliness and the majesty of the Kyles of Butte which provided a truly fitting close to the war which had brought us so much of ugliness and despair. It was as if we were being given a second lease on life, by its beauty and splendour.

I still had to wait for my second chance. My continued pleas fell on deaf ears; my dreams of attending university seemed far from reality; I was stuck in Niobe, indefinitely, it seemed.

Helping to demobilize the navy brought me some peculiar tasks. For example, I became the master window-repairman of Niobe. Over a period of weeks, I replaced hundreds of broken panes in windows which hadn't been touched throughout the war. I also became the master baggage-controller, seeing that every homeward-bound sailor ended up on his ship with all his luggage. (This task, at least, had a perk: instead of sleeping in the Nissen hut, I had a bunk tucked away in the baggage-room loft. It was snug, not subject to captain's rounds, ideal for reading late in the night.)

In between these priority jobs, I roamed the banks of the Clyde into Greenock, Gourock, Dumbarton, Clydebank and Glasgow, and even managed to reach Edinburgh. I roamed the moors and devoured book after book in the Niobe library. And I kept hoping for the news that I was going home. A welcome break in the routine in Niobe was the arrival of Sir Percy Noble, Commander-in-Chief of the Western Approaches; a man widely respected by all of us for his thorough knowledge of the movements of every ship in the war in the North Atlantic. He wanted one last

contact with all his old veterans. As he paraded up and down our lines, he expressed concern that none of us was wearing a single campaign ribbon, despite having been in the thick of it during all the war years. Before he left, he commanded us to wear them proudly—and so we did.

In early October, a delightful surprise: the entire crew of the Caraquet, including the captain, arrived in Niobe, homeward bound after decommissioning our beloved ship in Sheerness. They were astounded to find me still in Niobe, and the skipper said he would do his best to get me back with the crew for immediate return to Canada. Days passed without any sign of success, but at last he arrived with word that the captain of Niobe had reluctantly agreed to let me go. I literally jumped for joy.

Then came the day when all of us homeward-bound sailors lined up on the east lawn for the farewell address from the captain of Niobe. We were then trucked down to the Princess Docks in Greenock, and ferried out to the aircraft carrier H.M.C.S. Puncher, where we were hoisted aboard. The 10,000-ton ship was a madhouse of hundreds of sailors, soldiers and airmen; all were in an exultant mood, knowing that home was close at last. I was lucky enough to get a bunk, but most of the men were set up in three-tier metal beds, welded to the steel deck of the emptied hangar, now cleared of aircraft.

Followed by the hooting of all the nearby ships, we slipped out of Greenock and down the Clyde to the open sea. We gradually made our way between Scotland and Ireland, visible on both sides in the gathering twilight, then headed out into the open Atlantic. The Puncher settled down to a cruise that made the previous five-and-a-half years of life on corvettes seem as unreal as a bad dream. On the Puncher, we were passengers: crowded, yes, but passengers all the same. We could sleep, eat, listen to concerts by the Niobe band (which was heading home with us), read, play bridge, and give a lot of thought to our futures.

The meals were good, although we had to start lining up for lunch almost as soon as we had finished breakfast; and, all in all, we thought we had it made.

The first days were like an endless party, as we cruised along in moderate seas with the prevailing winds aft. Then the weather changed rapidly; and even the Puncher, with all her bulk and stability, began to roll and pitch like a giant Kamsack or Caraquet. The jubilant atmosphere vanished, as many of the men, particularly the soldiers and airmen, succumbed to seasickness. To make matters worse, dozens of the metal beds in the hangar tore loose from their weldments during the peak of the storm, tossing many of the men onto the deck and causing a number of injuries.

The weather cleared and our spirits began to revive again.

For me, the greatest pleasure was, of course, walking. I covered many a mile across the Atlantic on the flight deck of the Puncher. It was a half-mile around the deck, with a sheer drop to the ocean below the unprotected edges. All day long, mile after mile after mile, I walked, sometimes alone, sometimes in a group, either chatting or just looking out on the rolling seas of the now peaceful North Atlantic. The talk was always of home. As we came in on Cape Race, Newfoundland, we could almost smell land; then, it was down the coast of Nova Scotia, off Sambro Light, and, finally, into a bitterly cold and raw Halifax.

The greeting was far from cool. The docks were jammed with thousands of welcoming people, officers, enlisted men, friends, relatives, sweethearts. Bands were playing, flags were flying, and everywhere there was a spirit of joy and happiness.

We sailors were all bundled off to H.M.C.S. Peregrine, the demobilization barracks. The rest of the Caraquet's crew had their discharge papers all in order, and were ready to head home after medicals and the inevitable lecture about facing civilian life again.

But where were my papers? Nowhere to be found. Would I be held back yet again? No! My papers had been prepared months before, when I was first sent to Niobe. When I didn't show up in Halifax back in August, someone had tossed the papers aside, and they had been gathering dust in some corner of the vast processing unit ever since. Luckily they were unearthed and, for the last time, I rejoined my shipmates for the final haul.

First, came the painful process of saying farewell to the Guildfords, the Halifax family who had adopted more stray sailors during the war than the rest of Halifax put together. This wonderful family had fed, clothed and provided comfortable beds for sailors like myself throughout the war. We who found our way to the Guildfords—and it was an ever-widening group of sailors from all parts of Canada—would always treasure their warmth and concern for the men who returned from the sea, and their deep sorrow and dismay when they heard about those who would never return. I also had time to drop in on the Nebbs, the other family with whom I had sometimes stayed. They, and the Guildfords, had made Halifax a home port always to be treasured.

My last night in naval barracks brought an appropriate final task: duty watch. I found myself in charge of fire patrols, and once again, but for the last time, I got through the long hours between midnight and 0400. Then, later that day, it was back to the Halifax train station, packed with sailors, soldiers and airmen waiting to head off across Canada to their home towns. We caught the old D.A.R. Railway across Nova Scotia to Digby, crossed the Bay of Fundy on the Princess Louise, and then came the biggest shock of our naval careers.

Sitting in the railway station in Saint John, all arranged and waiting for us, was a special train, all sleeper coaches, each with berths made up with crisp white sheets and pillowcases; each with porters, ready to show us to our berths. For us veterans it was the most luxurious train trip imaginable: sleeping in clean, quiet surroundings after the turmoil of mess decks; eating full-course meals served on white tablecloths in the dining car; travelling in a style we never knew existed during the long years of war. It was as if the navy had decided to make up for what we had endured with this small taste of luxury. We enjoyed every moment.

When we changed in Montreal, a special train was waiting for us once again. As we headed across northern Ontario in late October, 1945, the snow was already heavy in the forests, and over the lakes and rivers; it was quite a sight for a lot of homesick sailors to see all that beauty while relaxing in comfortable coaches after a good breakfast.

Then came the sad part: the final stretch into Winnipeg and my stammered farewells to old shipmates continuing across the Prairies and on to the West Coast. I knew few of us would ever meet again. A last wave; a last goodbye and I descended the train steps.

Winnipeg. I was home.

There was no band, no welcoming committee; but it was still a wonderful moment: to return to the old home town after a terrible war; to return in one piece, with many memories to share and tales to tell; and to think about a boundless future, full of possibility. A lot had changed. The old neighbourhood looked different, and many of the young people I had known would never be coming home. But it was good to face this change. It was part of life, as it still is.

My last function in the navy took place in the local naval barracks, where, after a few good wishes for the future, a young sub-lieutenant handed over my official discharge papers. For the record, it was November 23, 1945.

The Department of Veterans Affairs was keen to help us rejoin civilian life. To my delight, I learned that I had been accepted at the University of Manitoba for a special first year, starting in January. (University terms generally begin in the fall.) For most of us veterans, the first two years of university were an endless struggle to keep up with youngsters just out of high school, but we did it.

How did we do it? Well, that's another story!

Photograph Credits

Public Archives of Canada: pages 1, 7, 24, 28, 30, 32, 35, 36, 37, 39, 40, 56, 61, 71, 78, 85, 86, 90, 93, 95, 98, 99, 104, 129.

Department of National Defence: pages 9, 38, 46, 47, 59, 130.

Author: pages 21, 69, 70, 77, 92, 105, 126, 140, 143.